DEVIL'S ADVOCATE

Devil's Advocate

THE UNTOLD STORY

KARAN THAPAR

HarperCollins *Publishers* India

First published in India in 2018 by
HarperCollins *Publishers*
A-75, Sector 57, Noida, Uttar Pradesh 201301, India
www.harpercollins.co.in

2 4 6 8 10 9 7 5 3 1

Photos courtesy of the author

P-ISBN: 978-93-5277-984-0
E-ISBN: 978-93-5277-985-7

The views and opinions expressed in this book
are the author's own and the facts are as reported by him,
and the publishers are not in any way liable for the same.

The 'Sunday Sentiments' columns on pp. 149–154. 166–167, 169–171, 172–175 and
195–197 have been reproduced with permission from the *Hindustan Times*.

Karan Thapar asserts the moral right
to be identified as the author of this work.

Typeset in 12/15.8 Bembo
Manipal Digital Systems, Manipal

Printed and bound at
Thomson Press (India) Ltd.

MIX
Paper
FSC FSC® C010615

This book is produced from independently certified FSC® paper to ensure
responsible forest management.

For Mummy, Daddy, Waffles and Abo

CONTENTS

1

MY UNEXPECTED ARRIVAL

I'm not sure if it was a bright and sunny day in Srinagar, but 5 November 1955, the day I was born at twenty minutes to 9 in the morning, was a Saturday. My arrival was not what my parents had expected—after three daughters and twenty years of trying and failing to have a son, they were convinced that I would be another girl. In fact, they had already arranged to leave their 'fourth daughter' and a nanny with my grandmother when they would depart six weeks later for a year in London.

Mummy was even reluctant to accept either the doctor's word or Daddy's that she'd finally had a boy. She thought they were hiding the truth from her. So as soon as she got a moment on her own, she undid my nappy to check for herself. Unfortunately, she got caught in the act and was mercilessly teased thereafter!

Once my parents accepted the fact that their long-sought-after son had arrived, everything changed. The nanny, Abo, and I were part of the family that sailed from Bombay. This little anecdote is an example of the upbringing I have had and, for some, an indication of the sort of person I would grow up to be.

My eldest sister Premila, who was a year old when Abo first joined us, couldn't pronounce the nanny's proper name, Dharmo Devi. And her married name, Havaldarni Khazan Singh Salaria, was even more complicated. So Premila called her Abo and the name stuck. In turn, Abo taught me to call Premila Bobo, the Dogri word for elder sister!

I adored Abo, as did my three sisters, Premila, Shobha and Kiran. By the time I was born she'd been with us for nearly twenty years. By the time she died it was over half a century. All four of us were brought up by her and I guess each one was spoilt in the same way. But I suspect that my relationship with her was different, for one significant reason. By the time I was born, my parents were a lot older, and that accounted for the difference. Daddy was a senior general in the Indian Army, commanding XV Corps. The demands on their time meant that I was placed more in Abo's charge than my sisters had been when they were young.

Abo would wash, scrub and dress me. She'd supervise my eating. At night I'd insist on sleeping in her bed. Except for the fact that she wasn't, she was like a mother to me.

When I was young, I often wondered why my parents had named me Karan. One of the explanations given was that my third sister, Kiran, was determined that her brother should be called Karan. Perhaps she thought there was something apt about names that almost rhymed. But it turns out that the idea of calling me Karan was proposed by a dear friend of my mother, Maharani Tara Devi of Kashmir. During the years my parents spent in Srinagar, Mummy had become close to the maharani, who used to call her 'Generalni'. It was her idea that if the child my mother was expecting turned out to be a boy, he must be named after her son Karan Singh. In fact, when I received the G.K. Reddy award in 2018, Dr Karan Singh, who was presiding over the ceremony, regaled the audience with this story. As he put it: 'I'm to blame for his name!'

Given that my parents were quite old when I was born (Daddy was fifty), it was perhaps inevitable that I would be pampered. Rarely did Daddy scold, and there was nothing that he would deny me. He was unfailingly indulgent. He seemed to enjoy my occasional naughtiness, as if it was proof that his son was spirited and not a sissy.

There was, however, one occasion when I was five when he did try to discipline me. I'm not sure what I had done, but I remember sensing that he would not be forgiving. At the time, we were living in Army House in Delhi and he was the army chief. As I saw the anger on his face I scarpered out of the room, ran down the corridor and out of the house. Daddy ran behind me. When the guards on duty saw us, they joined the chase.

This hilarious situation ended when I stumbled in the garden, giving Daddy and the guards the opportunity to catch up. But instead of the slap I'd expected, he picked me up in his arms and roared with laughter. Even though my behaviour had been unforgivable, my spunk had won his admiration.

After I was packed off to boarding school at the age of eleven, it was usually Daddy whose eyes would fill with tears when I would walk into his room to say goodbye before every school term. The paradox of the situation would lift my downcast spirits. His parting words were always the same: 'Remember,' he would say, 'all work and no play makes Jack a dull boy.' I could never fathom why he thought his son was a tedious bookworm!

Mummy was different. She consciously attempted to make up for Daddy's softness by putting on a tough exterior. Consequently, although everyone could see that she adored her son, I knew she wouldn't forgive my pranks and lapses.

'You're ruining the boy!' she would admonish Daddy each time he laughed away my bad behaviour.

'Oh come on, Bimla, he's only a child!'

'And he'll remain one,' she would riposte, 'if he doesn't learn how to behave himself.'

I guess that's why I was put into school when I was barely two-and-a-half years old. Perhaps Mummy also feared that in the company of three older sisters, her precious son would start behaving like a girl. So the nuns at Loreto Convent, Tara Hall, Simla, were prevailed upon to take me into their kindergarten. This, of course, meant that I began my education as a convent-school boy!

I'm not sure how much I learned, but I'm told that my daily hollering would bring the school to a stop. Kiran, who was sitting for her Senior Cambridge exams at the time, was repeatedly summoned to calm me down. Mummy, however, was adamant about keeping me in school and, despite the chaos I created, I was unfailingly sent every day.

A few years later, when Daddy was the Indian ambassador in Afghanistan, I was admitted to the American School in Kabul. It was the only English-speaking educational establishment in the country. It was here that I acquired a fondness for peanut butter, which my parents put up with and which, consequently, I've retained all my life. However, Mummy didn't take too kindly to the Americanisms I picked up. She wasn't happy with the 'gee whizzes' and 'aw shucks' I would expostulate when I came home but, no doubt, she hoped I'd grow out of them. But as soon as she heard me pronounce aluminium as 'aloominun' she decided that the situation needed immediate rectification. There was no way she would let her little boy end up with a Yankee accent!

So I was packed off to Doon School in Dehradun. Mummy organized my departure with the exactitude of a sergeant major. At the time I almost thought she was happy to be rid of me. Daddy, on the other hand, took to his bed. He didn't demur, but he wasn't at all convinced that his little boy needed to be sent to boarding school.

I can't deny that I didn't like the idea at all. As I waited in the airport departure lounge, surrounded by my mother and sisters, the Indian Airlines manager, a well-built gentleman called Anwar Malik, came up and addressed me. He thought he was speaking to a happy eleven-year-old looking forward to a big change in his life. 'Well, young man, everything under control?'

'Yes,' I bawled. 'Everything but my tears.'

∾

Whoever said that schooldays are the best days of your life was more than an ordinary pessimist. Logically, he must have been close to suicide!

These days I look back upon Doon with fondness and nostalgia but as a schoolboy I wasn't exactly ecstatic to be there. Of course, I would never have admitted it; that wouldn't have been the done thing. But every time the school train would pull out of New Delhi railway station at the start of another term, I would mentally compose a letter to my parents to tell them why I didn't want to continue at boarding school. The arguments I thought of were long, detailed and—or so I felt—undeniable. I was certain they were convincing.

The letter, however, never got written. Once I reached school, there was so much to do and so many friends to catch up with, I would postpone writing to the next day and then the day after that. Soon, so much time had elapsed that it felt silly to go ahead. 'I'll do it next term,' I would promise myself. But that day never came. I guess the charms of the school's seventy-acre Chandbagh estate, nestling in the Doon Valley and just fourteen miles from Mussoorie as the crow flies, eventually captivated every student no matter how homesick. It made you forget home and become completely immersed in your tasks at school. Since every boy was in the same boat, you soon learnt to sail together.

To tell the truth, I was a bit of a nerd at school. I knew I was undistinguished at sport and never tried to prove otherwise. Be it cricket, hockey or football, I carefully and deliberately kept away. And let me admit, I'm confident that that could only have helped the school or my house team!

My interests were not just non-athletic but individualistic. I acted, debated and took part in elocution competitions. I joined the editorial board of the school weekly and, eventually, rose to become its chief editor. Yet in all of this, I was unashamedly competitive. In my mind I was running a race and always wanted to be both first and best.

Vikram Seth, who was three years my senior and the Jaipur House debating captain, attempted to teach me the tricks of his trade. Seated cross-legged on a rickety wooden school chair, not unlike a meditating Buddha, he'd make me endlessly repeat a speech I had been told to learn by heart. As I did so, he would listen intently with his eyes screwed shut.

'Put more feeling into what you're saying,' he would occasionally interrupt. 'Your delivery has to make people listen to you. At the moment you sound like a broken-down record player.' When I tried to do as he said, Vikram would swiftly change his mind and say, 'Don't be so dramatic. You're sounding hysterical. Stop overdoing it.' However, when I tried to achieve the elusive golden mean, all I could get out of him was: 'Hmmm ... let's start again.' And so we would go on and on and on.

Vikram would literally wear one out. But I guess practice makes perfect. If nothing else, this ensured that Jaipur House team members knew their speeches so well that even stage fright on the night of the inter-house competition couldn't drive them out of our minds. Perhaps this is also why today, I have an infinite capacity to learn by rote. Alas, once the need to remember is over, I seem to forget pretty promptly too.

If not at the time then years later, as a television anchor, I realized the value of Vikram's instructions. Speaking carefully and deliberately, and learning to pause for effect, can often make the difference between an effective presentation on screen and a garbled one. However, what Vikram didn't teach us—how could he, his aim was to ensure that we spoke fluently and effectively—is that sometimes, not saying anything at all is the most powerful statement you can make. And it's a particularly useful trick for an anchor. It often encourages guests to carry on talking till they end up saying things they never intended to.

∾

The 'low' point of my acting career in school was a performance of Bernard Shaw's *Arms and the Man*. Another Vikram—this time Raja Vikram Dhar—was Sergius, the intended hero. I was Louka, the maid. Instead of falling for the beautiful and eligible daughter of the house, Sergius falls in love with the flirtatious maid. This misplaced romance reaches its climax when he embraces her. As Vikram Dhar sought to do so, the stockings I had worn started to fall. The more passionate he became, the faster they slid down to my ankles. Vikram, of course, was blissfully unaware of this denouement.

'Look, look, look, Vikram,' rose a loud, collective shout from hundreds of Doon School boys seated on the steps of the school's amphitheatre, known as the Rose Bowl. 'This girl's got horribly hairy legs. How can you kiss her?'

This so disconcerted Vikram that, forgetting himself, he looked down at my bare legs and visibly winced, before he resumed what he was supposed to be doing, which was embracing Louka. For the next few weeks Louka became my new name before, mercifully, everyone reverted to KT, my original nickname.

I've always been a bit reserved—or perhaps shy?—but at school, this did not prevent me from making firm and lasting friendships. The two friends who have stayed with me for decades thereafter are Praveen Anand, who was a year senior but later became my best man; and Analjit Singh, who was nicknamed Crack at school but whom I've always known as Manu. I have a third good friend, Prathik Malhotra, who was also at school with me but paradoxically, in those days we weren't close. At that time our worlds were rather different, although they've converged considerably since then. Today I see a lot of Pertie, as I call him, but I have few memories of things we did together at school.

I'm not sure why but in my last year, to my surprise—and, no doubt, to everyone else's dismay—my housemaster, Gurdial Singh, appointed me captain of Jaipur House. In those days it was exceptional for a non-sportsman to be chosen for this honour. I can only guess that perhaps Guru, as we fondly called him, was determined to show that there was more to achievement than sporting prowess.

At this point my dislike of boarding school gave way to the thrill of being house captain. After four years of being treated as a bit of a wimp—and laughed at because I couldn't kick a ball straight and had no idea how to hold a bat—it wasn't just unusual but exciting to be in a position to exercise power over my erstwhile detractors. Even though I tried to be modest, I can't deny that I enjoyed being top dog. Indeed, there must have been many occasions when that was blatantly obvious.

In the 1970s, the acme of achievement for most Doscos—as students of Doon School call themselves—was the sports blazer. It was what every sportsman wanted most of all. It also left the rest of us feeling both jealous and cheated because there was no equivalent for non-sportsmen. Then, in my last year, the headmaster of the day, Col. Eric Simeon, created an equivalent for scholars. He called it the scholar's blazer, which sounds odd but was rather appropriate because it was devised as a direct rival to the sports version. I was awarded the first one, which meant that I got to design what scholar's blazers would look like. At the age of fifteen, it was a heady experience.

The sports blazer was navy blue and double-breasted. Some people felt that the scholar's version should be markedly different. Red and single-breasted with three buttons was one suggestion, but it didn't appeal to me. I opted for a black double-breasted blazer. It was different from the sports blazer, but from a distance they were almost indistinguishable. I'm delighted that nearly fifty years have passed but the colour and style have stayed the same.

∾

In my time, most Doscos headed for college after finishing school. I ended up at another school. This time it was Stowe, a stunningly beautiful if academically undistinguished public school in England. My Senior Cambridge results had won me a scholarship to complete my A-levels in Britain, and Stowe became the first stage of what ended up as a long stay in that country.

Set in an eleven-hundred-acre estate just outside the little town of Buckingham, Stowe was not intended to be a school. It was built as the Duke of Buckingham's country seat. The architect was Sir John Vanbrugh and the gardens were landscaped by the famous Capability Brown. Later, both men combined to build Blenheim, but Stowe is aesthetically more disciplined and, therefore, a more pleasing product. If nothing else, every Stoic—the understandable if unfitting name that the school has given its students—leaves with an unparalleled experience of beauty. Eton and Harrow pale in comparison to the splendours of Stowe.

It was here that I first discovered and came to love English eccentricity. This was entirely because of Patrick Filmer-Sankey, a lanky, blond semi-aristocrat with whom I shared a study. His mother was the actress Adrienne Corri. No one ever spoke of his father and it was assumed that Patrick was illegitimate. I never asked and, consequently, was never told.

In 1972, the year I joined Stowe, Stanley Kubrick's film *A Clockwork Orange* was the big hit of the season. For many, its most striking scene is when Adrienne Corri is assaulted by the psychopath Alex. Few, if any, at Stowe brought this up in front of Patrick but on Saturdays, once classes were over, the media would descend on him, demanding to know what it was like to watch his mum being raped onscreen.

Patrick was utterly nonchalant. 'Honestly, old chap,' he would reply, 'no different to last week when you asked the same question.' The truth was that Patrick cared more about newts, his pet obsession, than his mother's recent if substantial fame. For the rest of Britain, the film was a popular watch. Patrick, however, pretended that he found it long and dull.

Patrick was also an incorrigible prankster. One Saturday night in summer, after picking the chapel keys out of the chapel prefect's pocket, he purloined the headmaster's secretary's Mini Cooper and drove it up fifty steps to the chapel entrance, then down the aisle and parked it where the altar was meant to be. The next morning, a Sunday, when the headmaster, Mr Drayson, strode in, followed in formal procession by the staff and students, he discovered a yellow Mini parked at the centre of the chapel nave. More than humiliated, the headmaster was apoplectic. The police were summoned, but they had no idea how to get the car out of the chapel. That's because no one could work out how it had got there in the first place. Patrick's ploy—which he kept a secret—had been to use the chapel kneelers to create a ramp over the stairs. The police, in ignorance but also in desperation, simply drove the car down bumpety-bump-bump over fifty stone stairs and wrote it off.

When eventually it was discovered that this was Patrick's handiwork, a livid headmaster decided to rusticate him and summoned Adrienne Corri to take him home. But that never happened. Using all the charm at her command—and she had pots of it—Adrienne not only talked Mr Drayson out of his decision but, more importantly for Patrick and me, into granting permission for her to take us out to lunch. As she put it: 'Now that I'm here and we've sorted this out, surely I can take the two boys out for a bite before I head back home?' Mr Drayson didn't have the heart to say no!

I grew to love Stowe. The enchantment of the estate was the first attraction. You could walk around for hours, visiting the quaint but wonderful monuments that dotted the landscape, passing sheep gambolling on the other side of a vast eight-acre lake, then on towards rarely visited and now, sadly, crumbling castles on distant, forgotten ridges. Away from the school yet surrounding it, this was another world. Every evening before supper it became my escape. I did a lot of growing up during these solitary walks.

The other great influence was the school's senior tutor, Brian Stephan, a puce-faced, crusty and taciturn man, whom many found difficult to relate to. In my case he became a mentor.

Mr Stephan taught me English literature and the constant challenge of trying to impress him seemed to bring out the best in me. He spoke very little, usually in monosyllables and always softly. So his praise meant a lot, assuming you could hear it! He encouraged me to sit for the Oxbridge entrance exam during the fourth term of my A-levels and not wait till I had finished them, as most students would. It was a daunting task, but he encouraged me to take it on.

That I got into Cambridge was perhaps entirely because of Brian Stephan. I owe him a huge debt of gratitude. However, luck played an almost equally important part. Even today, more than forty years later, I can hardly believe what happened at my interview. It took place on a cold, grey, blustery autumn afternoon in 1973. I can vividly recall it.

The porters at Pembroke College directed me to the room where I was expected. The door was ajar. Was that an invitation to walk in or simply carelessness? Unsure, I knocked. A loud but distant voice responded, 'Come in.'

I entered a square room lined with bookshelves up to the ceiling. The curtains were drawn and the lights were not bright. The rich smell of cigar smoke hung in the air. It was a comfortable, well-used room; but it was empty.

'I'm in the bath.' It was the same voice. 'Sit down and amuse yourself. I'll join you shortly.'

That was how Michael Posner, the man who was going to interview me and who would later become my tutor, introduced himself. I would learn more of his eccentric ways in the years to come, but upon this first encounter I was flummoxed. I had come prepared for a daunting interview. Although anxious, eager and excited, I was ready for almost anything—but not this.

At the age of seventeen, I wasn't sure what to do. I wanted to behave like an adult, but what would that amount to? I reached for a book and, standing by an old brass lamp, glanced at its pages. I can't remember its name but it was something to do with the Indian economy.

'Ah, there you are.'

I turned to find Mr Posner bearing down on me. He was a large man with an equally generous smile. He thumped my shoulder and more or less simultaneously pushed me into a large armchair. Then he sat down in another in front of me.

'What's that?'

Mr Posner reached for the book I had just put down. He seemed to know it.

'Well, young man, you want to come up to Pembroke, do you?'

'Yes, Mr Posner.' What else could I have said? The answer should have been obvious.

'In that case, what can you tell me about the Indian economy?'

It was a trick. Worse, I had created the opening for it by choosing that particular book. I wished I had picked up a magazine or a newspaper instead. Now I had to talk about a subject of which I was completely ignorant.

Inwardly I panicked, but outwardly I started to gabble. It was the only way of covering up. I must have spoken for three minutes or more.

'Hmmm.' The sound was enough to stop my flow. Posner was staring at the documents in his hand. I guessed that they must be part of my application form.

'Not knowing the subject doesn't seem to be a handicap for you!'

Ouch! Yet there was a hint of a smile and his eyes were gleaming. That was the first time I saw Posner embarrass and applaud in the same sentence. It was his trademark style. But on that dreary October afternoon, this was also the first suggestion that Pembroke would accept me. To this day I'm convinced that it was my ability to carry on speaking glibly even when I was not sure of what I was actually trying to say that did the trick. Incidentally, this has stood me in good stead ever since.

2

THE CAMBRIDGE UNION SOCIETY, AND MEETING BENAZIR

I arrived in Cambridge on an unusually warm and sunny October day. It's what the British call an Indian summer. This bright start was an accurate harbinger of what was to follow. My three years at Cambridge, supposedly studying economics and political philosophy, were exhilarating.

To begin with, I had no idea of what to expect. Although several cousins and uncles had been at the university and shared their stories, for me, each day was new and full of pleasant surprises. Looking back, this was probably because I was at an age when I was beginning to understand myself and realize what I was capable of.

More than academics, my interests and ambition were focused on the Cambridge Union Society. Unlike other universities, at Oxford and Cambridge the Union, though a student body, is not the students' union. It's the university's debating society and its membership is far bigger and more sought after.

The Cambridge Union Society was founded in 1815, almost a decade before its Oxford counterpart. It has a chamber similar to the House of Commons and although by the 1970s white tie had given way to black, Union debates still felt like special occasions. To be president of the Union was—and still is—considered a commendable achievement. Several British prime ministers won their political spurs as presidents of one or the other Union. But the Cambridge Union can also boast of names that are more easily recognized internationally, such as the economist John Maynard Keynes; Arianna Huffington née Stassinopoulos, the co-founder of *Huffington Post*; and the bestselling author Robert Harris.

If I recall correctly, three Indians had been elected to the presidency of the Cambridge Union before me. One of them was the lawyer, diplomat and governor Shanti Swaroop Dhavan. Another was his son Rajeev. They were, possibly, the first father-son combination to make it to the top. The third was the former minister Mohan Kumaramangalam. As an undergraduate, Jawaharlal Nehru was a member but no more. As prime minister, he became one of the few world leaders to be accorded honorary membership.

My career at the Union was the result of a fortuitous accident. It happened when, on my first day at Pembroke, still unsure and uncertain of my new surroundings, I met someone who went on to become one of my closest friends. His name was Satish Agarwal or, as he used to pronounce it with the Midlands accent he had picked up in Nottingham, Saytish Uggerwall. Born in Moga, in rural Punjab, Satish had grown up and been schooled in the English Midlands. Despite his appearance, he belonged more to Robin Hood's Nottingham than the Punjab his parents had left behind.

We took to each other immediately and when he told me he had just joined the Union, I decided that I would too. I was literally being a copycat; I had no better reason than that.

I got my break at the Union during the annual Freshmen's Debating Competition. The motion was 'This House prefers Marks & Spencer to Spencer and Marx'. I was given the daunting task of opposing it. Although Edward Mercer, a tall, freckled, chestnut-haired undergraduate from Trinity, came first, and I only second, to my surprise I ended up attracting more attention.

My career at the Union got an initial boost and succeeded because of two serendipitous misunderstandings and one undeniable fact that stood me in good stead. I used to joke about this at the time, but the more I reflect on it, the more I suspect it is also the truth.

First, my name 'Karan' led most undergraduates to assume it was a misspelling of the female Christian name 'Karen'. So, many who didn't know me thought that I was a girl! They felt it would be fun to vote for one.

The second misunderstanding arose out of my manner and, possibly, from the obvious interest I took in my sartorial appearance. This led several to believe that I was fey. Some even went the whole hog and thought that I was gay! Either way, rather than put people off, this made me stand out, which in turn attracted attention and, from some, support.

The undeniable fact I benefited from is that I look Indian. 'Wogs' in those days were still a bit of an oddity at the Union. Perhaps they still are. But in the mid-1970s, to find one climbing the ladder was so uncommon that it felt unique. For this reason alone, I seemed a cause worth supporting!

After three consecutive terms on the Standing Committee, a defeat in my first bid for secretary but success in the second, I was unopposed for vice-president and thereafter for the presidency. So, in the Lent Term of 1977, I became president of the Union. At twenty-one, this was an intoxicating experience.

Even though my final Tripos exams were just months away and I had only a faltering grasp on my subject, political philosophy, for the duration of my presidency, nothing mattered more than the Union. Looking back after forty years, which is ample time to put things in perspective and shed my juvenile euphoria, two events—and one sparkling political guest—stand out.

The first, almost at the start of my presidential term, was one of the most unusual events the Union has ever staged—a Ravi Shankar concert in King's College Chapel.

On a cold, snowy January night, without any heating in the chapel (because the Union couldn't afford to pay for it), Ravi Shankar performed in front of over a thousand people. Even though he sat on a platform six inches above the chapel's stone floor, he was still freezing. This meant that he had to play vigorously just to keep himself warm. The energy that produced added unbelievably to his performance. It started at 8 p.m. and carried on well past midnight.

Afterwards, we took Ravi Shankar, Allah Rakha—the renowned tabla player accompanying him—and the tanpura player Pradyot Sen to the Union for supper. After the chilly chapel, they were hoping for something hot and were horrified by the spartan, cold repast they were offered. None more so than Allah Rakha, who found sausages mixed in with the crumb-fried chicken wings.

'Don't you know I'm Muslim?' he thundered.

'I'm really sorry,' I stammered. 'I forgot about that.'

'How could you? With a name like Allah Rakha how could you have forgotten that I'm Muslim?'

He had a fair point. So absorbed had I been in arranging the finances, publicity and audience to ensure that the concert would be a success, I'd completely overlooked the fact that the artistes would want a proper meal before they headed back to London, and that one of them was obviously Muslim. I'm afraid my lack of attention to detail left them starving!

The second event that had me cock-a-hoop was more conventional—it was a debate. But it was the motion I concocted that truly pleased me. This was for the funny debate of term. Each term the Union has one. However, as I realized over the years, finding a genuinely witty motion becomes increasingly difficult. Which was why I was so proud of mine: 'A drink before and a cigarette after are three of the best things in life!' It was enough to get the speakers going. We had a hilarious time as people sought to identify the missing third element. The next day's *Times Diary*, written by the then famous 'PH simplyguessverk'—the idiosyncratic generic name used by the paper's diarist—was entirely devoted to a lengthy account of the night.

The guest I will never forget was the Liberal Party leader of the time, Jeremy Thorpe. He accepted my invitation to propose the motion 'Politics is an honourable profession' in December, several weeks before the start of the Lent term. However, by the time the date arrived, he was caught in the middle of a dreadful controversy that threatened his career. Thorpe had been accused of attempting to murder his alleged homosexual lover and the grim details surrounding this episode, as well as the growing question mark about his future, dominated the news.

I expected Thorpe to cancel. Fortunately, he saw this as an opportunity to prove that he was undeterred and determined to carry on. So he turned up. At the time there weren't any paparazzi, but the behaviour of the press was no different. Hundreds of journalists, cameramen and photographers crowded the platform at Cambridge's little railway station as the train carrying Thorpe arrived. From that moment, I knew that this debate would be at the top of the night's news bulletins and on the next morning's front pages. Thorpe's predicament gave the Union the sort of publicity it yearned for.

I thought that the hullaballoo would continue all night and, indeed, well into the next morning, because Thorpe had chosen to stay overnight in Cambridge. But to my surprise, the media throng melted away as soon as the debate was over. No doubt this was because Jeremy Thorpe did not drop his guard. The media had been hoping that he would wilt, perhaps even break down, but nothing of the sort happened. Instead, his fortitude in the face of adversity put him into a ridiculously good mood. So after the debate, around 11 p.m., I invited him to my digs for a drink. He readily accepted and soon we were settled in my ground-floor room on Pembridge Street, opposite Pembroke College, swigging sherry, because that's all I had to offer.

Several friends who lived in the same building joined us. The spontaneous group included my sister Kiran and brother-in-law Irwin, who were visiting for the occasion. This gave Jeremy Thorpe the audience he needed and, therefore, he played to the gallery. All politicians are showmen and Thorpe was one of the best. Controversy had forced him to restrain himself but now, in convivial company and after several glasses of Tio Pepe, he was happy to reveal his normal jovial self.

As the clock struck 1, Thorpe started to perform padmasana. Once that was over he regaled us with stories, truthful if indiscreet, about all his opponents at the House of Commons. Each was more revealing than the last.

Hacks always want to be close to politicians and this was a God-given opportunity, more than I could have hoped for or even imagined. By the time Thorpe decided to call it a night, he left behind a room full of admirers. I'm convinced every one of them still has a soft corner for him though, shortly thereafter, his career ended in disgrace and he lived the rest of his life in quiet retirement.

∾

It was because of the Union that I got to know, and became close friends with, Benazir Bhutto. Although we became presidents of the

Cambridge and Oxford Unions at the same time (the Lent Term of 1977, which at Oxford is known as the Hilary Term), our first meeting had happened a few months earlier. At the time she was the treasurer of the Oxford Union and I was the vice-president at Cambridge, where she had come to propose the motion 'This house would have sex before marriage'. For an aspiring Pakistani politician, this was dangerous territory to tread on, but at the time it just felt like a fun debate.

I remember that night's events as if they had happened yesterday. Benzair was wearing a sea-green chiffon Mukaish saree. Those days, Pakistanis had no inhibitions in wearing sarees. She also had short, dark-brown hair and glasses perched on her hooked nose.

Benazir was in full flow at the despatch box when I pressed the president's bell. It was a breach of Cambridge Union protocol because the bell is only for the president to use and no one else. Unaware of this, she turned and looked at me expectantly.

'I see, madam, that you're proposing sex before marriage. Would you care to practise what you preach?' It was sophomore humour, but it had everyone in fits of laughter and I was, consequently, rather pleased with my intervention.

Cleverly, Benazir waited for the laughter to subside. Then she ostentatiously whipped off her glasses, screwed up her nose and responded: 'Certainly, but not with you!' She got an even bigger round of applause.

Strange as it may seem, this introduction led to a firm and lasting friendship. Benazir was staying at the Garden House Hotel, not far from Pembroke, so after the debate we walked back together. I invited her to my rooms for a cup of coffee before escorting her to the hotel and she agreed.

At the time, Benazir was a spontaneous and fun person, though extremely conscious of whose daughter she was and the fact that her having an Indian friend could be misunderstood or, at least, misrepresented in Pakistan. That meant that there was always a touch of tension in our friendship.

Weeks later, when we were both presidents of our Unions, we invited each other to participate in debates. She returned to Cambridge to oppose the motion 'That art is elitist—or it is nothing'. Yehudi Menuhin, Clive James and Arianna Stassinopoulos were some of the other speakers on that occasion.

In turn, Benazir invited me for her presidential debate when she was retiring as president. These debates are occasions to praise the retiring officer and to laugh and have fun. So I thought of a little joke. I gifted her a book. 'Given how popular you are,' I said, 'the book I'm giving you could well be your biography. It's called *All the President's Men!*'

'Hmm…' she responded. 'If the rest of your speech is as bad as your start, perhaps I should ask you to stop and sit down!'

However, the evening was overshadowed by one of her Australian friends whose attempt to embarrass Benazir was far superior to mine. The year was 1977 and unknown to any of us, her father was destined to fall from power a few months later. But at the time, he was still prime minister of Pakistan.

When it was the Australian gentleman's turn to speak—I can't remember his name; history always forgets the secondary player—he rose, cleared his throat and launched into a well-prepared but significantly altered version of *'Don't cry for me, Argentina'*.

'Don't cry for me, Islamabad.
The truth is I never left you.
All through my wild days, my mad existence, I kept my promise.
Don't keep your distance…'

This had the audience literally rolling in the aisles. The allusion was obvious and the joke, though made in fun, telling. Following the March elections, ferment had already started in Pakistan. Although the end was still unpredictable, the comparison with Eva Perón was stinging.

'Thank you, sir,' Benazir interrupted, enforcing her prerogative as president to catch the speaker off-guard. 'Every queen is entitled to a court jester, but if you're looking for a job, I suggest you try the Goon Show instead. I already have enough fools around me.'

Shortly thereafter, both universities shut for the Easter vacation. For undergraduates like Benazir and me, who would face our final exams in just two months, it was time to buckle down and study. This was our chance to make up for all the work that had been sacrificed whilst we were presiding over our respective Unions. So I was quite surprised when suddenly, over the Easter weekend, Benazir phoned to ask if she and a friend—Alicia, if my memory is correct— could visit Cambridge. There was little chance I would say no and, fortunately, there were a few empty rooms in my digs because their occupants had gone home on holiday.

Unfortunately, it was a tense time for Benazir. Her father's electoral victory a few weeks earlier, amidst widely believed allegations of rigging, had sparked widespread opposition protests which seemed to grow day by day. To control them, her father was forced to progressively declare what amounted to martial law. The British press was critical of him.

Benazir spent a lot of her time glued to my little transistor. The BBC World Service news was the most informed way of following developments in South Asia. It was also a lot easier than visiting the common room to watch TV; she knew that there, most of the others would be watching her instead.

On their last night in Cambridge, Benazir and Alicia decided to cook. I can't remember what they served but later, after coffee, Benazir suddenly decided that we should drive to London in her little MG for Baskin-Robbins ice cream. And that's precisely what we did. Squeezed into her little car, we set off around 10 p.m. and returned well past midnight. I think this was her way of breaking free from the pall of gloom the dismal news from Pakistan had spread upon all of us.

The next morning, before she left, she handed me a present. It was a 45 rpm record she had brought with her. One of the two songs was *'You're more than a number in my little red book'*. But what she said was more pointed: 'I bet you'll tell the whole world about this and make it seem more than it is!' And then, laughing, she added: 'And when you do, I'll know you're just a wretched Indian.'

That summer Benazir finished Oxford and returned home to Pakistan, intending to join her country's Foreign Service, but after her father was deposed in a coup, she entered politics instead and, finally, became prime minister. I chose to move to Oxford.

Neither then nor now am I clear about why I did this. The best answer is that with the Emergency imposed in India, I was reluctant to return. But it's also true that I hadn't done much to find a job. So three more years at Oxford, purportedly researching for a DPhil, seemed to be the easy option.

When I visited St Antony's for my admission interview, Benazir, who had arranged for us to have lunch afterwards and had come to pick me up, was the one who first told me that I would get in. This was virtually as soon as I walked out of a pretty forbidding questioning, where I didn't think I had excelled myself.

'I think you're in,' was the first thing she said when we met. 'That old white-haired man who walked out of the room before you did, told the lady sitting beside me who I think is his secretary, "Tick his name." So you're in.'

Benazir turned out to be right. The three years at Oxford that followed were completely different to the three before at Cambridge. For a start, I was no longer an irresponsible undergraduate. At the time, St Antony's was a very modern college without a history of hallowed traditions. All the students were graduates, most were married and several had children. There was no high table but a cafeteria system instead. Meal times were a mad family picnic. Finally, there were more foreign students than English.

I enjoyed Oxford, but I have to admit that I wasn't very serious about my research. Though I did a fair amount, I'm not sure whether my diligence was rewarded with distinguished results.

Instead, I started to write. Alexander Chancellor was the editor of the *Spectator* and he accepted several of my pieces. He even commissioned a visit to Afghanistan, shortly after the Soviet invasion of December 1979, which gave me my first cover story.

This was enough to convince me that I wanted to be a journalist, not an academic. So, shortly before completing three years at Oxford and long before completing my DPhil thesis (which remains un-submitted to this day), I wrote to six different newspapers, asking if they would take me on. The result was not just my first job but the start of the only career I've ever known.

3

CHARLIE, AND MY FIRST JOB

Of the six newspaper editors I wrote to, four didn't bother to respond while one wrote a rather rude reply. However, the sixth letter, to *The Times*, led to a phone call from the paper's deputy editor, Charles Douglas-Home.

This was the summer of 1980 and in those days there were no mobile phones. Fortunately, there was a payphone just outside my room. Somewhat presumptuously, I had given this number in my letters, along with the college's main switchboard numbers.

'I can't remember when I last received such a cheeky letter!' Charlie began. I wasn't sure what to say, so I kept silent. 'I think we better have lunch so that I can discover what prompted this audacity.' I could hear Charlie chuckling. He was clearly enjoying this. He invited me to his London club, The Caledonian.

It wasn't my academic credentials, leave aside my conversation, that impressed Charlie at lunch. That happened because of sheer good luck. I was able to prove him wrong on a small but significant matter of fact. First, however, the lunch got off to a dreadful start.

I ordered haggis. 'You sure about that?' Charlie asked. 'Have you had it before?'

I hadn't, but I felt I could hardly admit to that. So I tried to bluff, claiming that I was familiar with it.

Alas, when the haggis was placed before me, the look on my face gave me away. 'Serves you right.' Charlie chuckled. I was getting used to his laugh. 'Now you better eat all of it.'

Charlie was a small man, with a round face and an irresistible smile. He was an aristocrat, but with a distinctly meritocratic and even egalitarian approach towards his colleagues. His father's elder brother was the fourteenth earl of Home, better known as Sir Alec Douglas-Home, who had served as the British prime minister as well as foreign secretary. Through his mother's side, Charlie was Princess Diana's father's first cousin, which made him her first cousin once removed.

Mercifully, Charlie was a chatty individual and our conversation soon distracted his attention from my earlier faux pas. 'You've done the opposite of Norman St John-Stevas, haven't you?' he suddenly asked.

At the time, St John-Stevas was one of Margaret Thatcher's ministers and a former president of the Cambridge Union. After three years at Cambridge, he had moved to Oxford to do a second degree. I had trodden a similar path.

'No,' I replied. 'I've done the same thing.'

'Hmm...' Charlie muttered. 'We'll go back to my office after lunch and check *Who's Who*.'

When we did, Charlie discovered I was right. Minutes later, he popped another of his famous questions: 'There's someone from India coming to see me tomorrow. Do you know the person?'

This really was an amazing question because, with the Indian population then approaching one billion, it was extremely unlikely that I would. 'I doubt it,' I said. 'But who's the person?'

Charlie opened his diary and said (although he mispronounced the name horribly): 'Nayantara Sahgal.' This was the last name I'd expected to hear. Aunty Tara, as I call her, is my mother's brother's wife, but I had no idea that she was in London and I could hardly believe Charlie had asked me about her.

Astonishment must have been written all over my face because he suddenly said, sounding somewhat incredulous, 'Do you know her?' When I said I did and explained how, he seemed inexplicably impressed.

I'm convinced that my handling of these idiosyncratic questions got me a job at *The Times*. Years later, when I knew Charlie better, I asked him up front. 'Don't be a fool,' he responded and laughed away my enquiry. But there was something about his manner that suggested I was right.

The Times needed to send someone to Nigeria immediately where, with a Second Republic inaugurated under President Shehu Shagari after years of military rule, they felt the need for a correspondent. Apparently, at a Mansion House banquet the night before, President Shagari had asked Charlie why *The Times* did not have a representative in Lagos. This must have been on the top of his mind when we met and perhaps he decided to fit me into a little vacancy that had just opened up.

I now faced a difficult choice. I could either complete my DPhil and forego the opportunity of joining *The Times*, because the paper would not keep the Lagos position open for long, or accept and hope to start a career but never finish my thesis. I opted for the latter and I've never regretted it. In my heart I knew I wasn't cut out to be an academic and Oxford had just been a way of postponing the real world.

I didn't realize how kind and thoughtful Charlie was until I started working for him. 'Don't file directly to the desk,' he told me when I left for Lagos. 'File to me instead.'

This was wise advice, because I was a novice and unaware of the pyramid structure a newspaper article needs to observe. But what took me by surprise was Charlie's response to the stories I filed.

Practically every night around 11, I would get a call from him. He would have the story I had filed earlier in the day and, like a diligent tutor, would point out my mistakes as well as the little 'tricks' I should deploy to make either my writing or the structure more riveting. These conversations could range between five minutes and twenty. I can't recall a single occasion when a story I filed was not followed by a late-night tutorial.

One day, after roughly three months, Charlie rang up in the morning. 'From today, I want you to file directly to the desk. Your copy is as good as any other correspondent's.' In his eyes I was now a proper journalist!

In the early 1980s, Nigeria was a rough place. Lagos, the capital, is in the heart of Yorubaland, where the people are tall, broad and loud. This part of the country felt like the American Wild West. The people seemed distinctly Texan.

As a new journalist, I lacked discrimination. I wasn't sure what was important and what should be considered irrelevant. I, therefore, ended up chasing every story, no matter how slight, and that often left me running around in circles.

On one occasion, however, I hit the bullseye without realizing that that's where I was heading. Through a series of lucky accidents, I played a critical role in Nigeria breaking diplomatic relations with Libya.

It happened on a slow and dull morning when I decided to attend a press conference at the Libyan Embassy because, quite frankly, there was nothing better to do. In a room that was barely full and where I was the only foreign correspondent, the ambassador started to speak. Shortly after he began, a door behind him opened and in marched five Libyan students who declared that they had taken over the embassy. They now proclaimed a 'jamhuriyat'. The announcement elicited desultory applause, followed by tea and biscuits.

Later that afternoon, I decided to visit the Nigerian Foreign Office. I was still trying to fill my day and didn't expect very much from this trip either. But it was when I asked the Foreign Office spokesman what he made of the morning's developments at the Libyan Embassy that I inadvertently pressed a Nigerian panic button.

'What!' he almost shouted. 'Are you sure this happened? You're not making it up, are you?'

'Yes, of course I'm sure,' I said. I couldn't understand why he was so worked up.

'Wait here. I must inform the minister.' And with that he ran out of the room and up six floors to the foreign minister's office. He was in such a hurry, it didn't occur to him to take the lift.

Half an hour later I heard him running down the stairs. 'Come with me quickly,' he shouted as he burst into the room. 'The minister wants to meet you.'

When I entered the sixth-floor office, it was like walking into an English Star Chamber. The foreign minister was seated on a raised chair at the far end. Flanking him on either side were the top officials of the ministry, the permanent secretary, the additional secretary, several undersecretaries and many others junior to them. I was left standing at the far end of a long table.

'Mr Thapar,' the minister addressed me in a deliberate and somewhat portentous voice, 'I'm told you have a story of the utmost importance to tell me.'

I repeated everything that had happened that morning at the Libyan Embassy. In fact, somewhat unnerved by the surroundings, I tried to recall the smallest details, no matter how insignificant. The minister listened intently. The accompanying officials kept their eyes focused on me right through. I felt like an accused standing in the dock.

'I see,' the minister said when I finished. 'Come back in two hours' time and you'll find that Nigeria is grateful for the service you've done.'

Unsure of what he meant and unaware of the alleged service I had performed, I wandered the streets outside the Foreign Office in a bit of a daze. When two hours were up, I returned to the spokesman's office and, once again in his company, was escorted to the minister's chambers.

It was the same scene that greeted me, except now there was less tension in the air. The minister seemed more relaxed.

'Mr Thapar, you have brought a very serious matter to our attention and I'm very grateful. As a reward, I'm going to give you a bit of news before anyone else finds out. Nigeria has decided to break relations with Libya. This is exclusive to you. The rest of the world will only find out tomorrow morning.'

I was stunned. I could hardly believe what I had just heard. Instead, my mind was flooded with questions. Why had this decision been taken? What had Libya done that was so unforgiveable? And what more was there to this story, because clearly there had to be? But before I could ask any of these questions I was marched out of the room by the spokesman, escorted down the stairs and bid farewell at the front door of the foreign ministry.

The Times could hardly believe my story when I filed my report. Charlie actually called to ask if I was hallucinating or bluffing. When he realized I wasn't, his conclusion was short, sweet and simple: 'You really are a lucky sod!'

Two days later I received a call from the Libyan Embassy, inviting me to a meeting with their foreign minister at 5 p.m. Apparently this gentleman had urgently flown in from Tripoli to make amends and restore relations. But his efforts had been in vain. By the time I met him, his frustration had turned to anger. For half an hour he ranted. I thought the veins on his forehead would burst. All the while he wagged his right index finger at me. Eventually, exhausted, he told me to 'get out'. But little did he realize he had just gifted me the perfect sequel to my scoop.

The second time I stumbled upon a big story in Lagos, it culminated in the end of my tenure as *The Times*'s correspondent in Nigeria. It happened late one night, a couple of days before I was anyway due to go on holiday. Returning from The Bagatelle, a Lebanese-owned French restaurant that had just been refurbished and was the fashionable place to visit, I found the Nigerian Foreign Office blazing like a towering inferno. Realizing at once that this was not the sort of thing a journalist encounters every day, I hurriedly dropped home the two people I had taken out to dinner and picked up the night guard from outside my own house before heading back to the burning ministry.

By now, there were a couple of fire brigades outside the building and a lot of firemen who seemed to be simply standing and watching. The burning building was, of course, an unbelievable sight to behold.

However, what caught my attention was a long fire hose that stretched from a centrally parked fire brigade, ran across the adjoining road and dipped into the sea, a distance of perhaps a hundred feet. There, with their feet in the water, a handful of firemen were pouring buckets of seawater into this limp pipe.

Of course, the other fire brigades did have Simon Snorkel ladders fixed to their roofs, each of which had risen to the level the fire was blazing at. No doubt they were addressing the problem adequately. But it was the farce at ground level that stuck in my mind.

So when I filed my report for *The Times* at around 1 in the morning, this was a part of the story. I didn't play it up but it stood out nonetheless.

The next morning, the story was on the paper's front page from where the BBC World Service programme *News of the African World* picked it up. Its first bulletin led with the disaster that had struck the Nigerian Foreign Office.

It didn't take long for officialdom in Lagos to work out that I was the journalist who had told the world about the fire. And, as I was soon to discover, this sort of luck doesn't stand a journalist in good stead. Even before offices formally opened, I received a summons to meet Chief Charles Igoh, President Shagari's chief press secretary.

Normally, Chief Igoh was a man given to much laughter. He would respond to the silliest of jokes with a long and exaggerated guffaw. On this occasion, however, he sat like a large, solid rock behind an imposing desk and refused to return my greeting when I walked into his office.

'Karan,' he began in a solemn voice, 'we had great hopes when you came but you've let us down. You're Indian, we're Nigerian, and we thought you would understand us. But I have to say I'm disappointed.'

'Why?' I asked hesitantly.

'Because you're as bad as the bloody British!'

'Chief Igoh,' I said unthinkingly, 'given that I work for a British paper that has to be a compliment.'

Chief Igoh wasn't amused. 'Why do I have to wake up and find out from you that my Foreign Office is on fire? Do you have nothing better to report?'

I tried to explain how this had happened but I soon realized he wasn't listening. So, when it was clear that the chief had finished, I politely but quietly got up and left.

After a week or so I flew out of Lagos for London and onwards to Delhi for my first long vacation in eighteen months. That's roughly how long I had been at my first job. A few days later, I got a call from Charlie.

'They've withdrawn your accreditation, which means they've effectively expelled you. They say you're welcome back in a private capacity to collect your belongings, but I've ruled that out. We'll have your things packed and returned to London. When you finish your holiday, I'll find something else for you to do.'

Thus ended my first and only stint as a foreign correspondent. What I didn't know at the time was that this would make it possible for me to join television and start a journey on a very different journalistic path.

4

MY WIFE, NISHA

Some of the best things in my life have happened by accident or, at any rate, unpredictably. My marriage was one of them. You could almost say that I was a guest who came over for a night and stayed forever!

It all started in October 1980, when I needed to spend a few days in London before moving to Lagos as *The Times*'s correspondent. I had an offer to stay with a dear friend, Vaneeta Saroop, but at the last minute, her landlady turned up and Vaneeta arranged for me to spend the first night with two sisters, friends of hers, living in the basement flat of her building.

So, with two large and bulging suitcases, I arrived at the front door of Nisha and Gita Meneses' flat. Gita, the elder sister, agreed to give me a bed for the night and put me up in Nisha's room without telling her.

Shortly after arriving, I showered and left for work. That evening when I returned, I could hear the sisters quarrelling. 'The next time you have a guest, give him your room,' I heard Nisha say. 'How dare you turf me out of mine!'

'Shush. He can hear you.'

Gita's attempts to silence her sister were unsuccessful and there was little doubt that I was the cause of the problem. Nisha wasn't at all pleased to see me.

For reasons I no longer remember, this unpropitious start was rapidly forgotten. In fact, even after Vaneeta's landlady left, I continued to stay with the Meneses sisters. At the time we were just friends in our carefree mid-twenties.

It was a holiday in London six months later that changed the relationship between Nisha and me. This time, Nisha invited me to stay and when I arrived, I found Gita away and the two of us on our own. Four weeks later, I proposed and Nisha said she'd give her answer in a few weeks' time.

Back in Lagos, I got caught in a swirl of political developments that seemed to threaten Nigeria's Second Republic. The Shagari government had lost its parliamentary majority and serious questions were being asked about the president's ability to handle this precarious situation. Many people thought his future looked bleak.

So when the phone rang late one night and Nisha began with the words 'Do you remember the question you asked me?', it was the last thing I'd expected to hear.

'What question are you talking about?' I foolishly and unthinkingly replied.

'You asked me to marry you and I'm ringing to say yes!' Fortunately, Nisha was laughing. She realized she'd caught me on the hop and saw the funny side of it.

Unfortunately, what should have been simple sailing thereafter turned into rather turbulent waters. Back in London after my 'expulsion' from Nigeria, I stayed with Nisha and Gita once again. By then I had come to know that this was actually Nisha's flat, where her sister was a guest like me. As Nisha's fiancé, I was no longer an interloper.

We fixed our marriage for December 1982 in Delhi, when both of us would be on holiday to meet our parents. This would ensure that both families could be present and all the celebrations arranged with typical Indian fanfare and festivity.

Meanwhile, Nisha and I started living together. It wasn't a secret, but Nisha had given her parents the impression that we weren't sharing a bedroom. They were Goan Catholics and therefore, this facade of propriety was important.

Unfortunately, sometime during the summer of 1982 Nisha got pregnant. It wasn't intended; it was an accident. Our marriage was about six months away and this was not an easy situation to handle. She knew it would upset her parents.

With the help of my close friend Praveen Anand, who at the time was with the Hammersmith Hospital and had also become a good friend of Nisha's, we arranged for an early termination of the pregnancy. Only a handful of our friends knew about this.

Alas, two months before our marriage, Gita decided to inform her parents. Nisha and I were never sure why she did this, but it came as a bolt out of the blue. It understandably upset Nisha's mother who, thereafter, was unshakably convinced that I had led her daughter astray.

In a moment of anger, Nisha's parents wrote to say that, under the new circumstances, they were no longer prepared to arrange our wedding in Delhi. This was a shattering blow. Nisha had wanted a traditional church ceremony and the fact that it could no longer happen, with her parents and friends around, was deeply hurtful. Fortunately, Mummy had no such concerns.

That left the two of us with a simple choice. The marriage had to take place in London and, thereafter, we would go to Delhi as a married couple. Strangely, her parents had no problem hosting a reception. In fact, they seemed rather keen to do that. The church wedding was where they drew the line.

Today, looking back, I'm actually thankful that events developed as they did because otherwise Father Terry Gilfedder would never have come into our lives. He was the parish priest at St Mary of the Angel's on Moorhouse Road, the local Catholic church, a short walk from Nisha's flat on Colville Road in Notting Hill Gate.

Father Terry agreed to officiate at our wedding. However, because Nisha wanted a church wedding, he was also required to put us through three formal 'instructions' prior to the event.

I suppose the terminology put me off. 'I'm damned if my kids will be forced into Catholicism,' I declared with misplaced passion. I can't recall how Nisha assuaged my temper but when we met Father Terry for the first of these sessions I was irritable, to say the least.

He offered sherry. I was taken aback. It was 6 in the evening and although I'm not averse to a tot, I hadn't expected this. Our conversation flowed like a river in torrent, sometimes loud and forceful, sometimes full and serene, occasionally like the rapids, short, sharp and staccato. We covered a range of subjects, but religion or Catholicism was not among them. I was enjoying myself. Father Terry filled my glass frequently and I drank without care.

The hour passed swiftly and when we rose to leave, Father Terry asked if next week at the same time would be convenient. I nodded and we were almost out of the door when his voice stopped us.

'I have a question and I wonder if you will answer it the next time,' he began. 'Why aren't the two of you living together?'

I'm not sure if the blood drained from our faces but we were speechless and stunned. We had lied and given Father Terry different addresses. Both Nisha and I thought that the truth should best be kept secret. After all, you don't tell a Catholic priest that you're living in sin!

This was Father Terry's disarming way of telling us that he knew and couldn't care less. It sealed our friendship. I was still twenty-six and for me he became the most enlightened man in the world.

Despite the fact that Nisha was marrying a Hindu, Father Terry agreed to a wedding with a full Catholic mass. At the time I didn't appreciate how unusual this was. I even failed to grasp the significance of his suggestion that I should choose one of the two readings from the Bhagavad Gita. In the end, since I was not that familiar with the book, I could not, so he chose one from Kahlil Gibran instead. I asked if this cross-cultural ecumenism was permitted by the church. I can never forget his reply.

'It's not where it comes from that matters,' he said. 'It's what it says that counts.'

However, it was Father Terry's sermon that will always linger as the lasting memory of our wedding. He didn't do what Catholic priests often do, which is to break into a discourse on fire and brimstone, God and damnation. Instead, using simple words of almost one syllable, he spoke of love. Nisha, our guests and I listened spellbound.

'Karan and Nisha,' he said, pronouncing our names with the gentle lilt of his Scottish accent, 'I want to speak of three little words: I love you. Three words that symbolize today's ceremony and your relationship with each other. Love is the bond that unites you but if you forget that you are two separate people, with separate habits, wishes and rights, love will also separate you. Never forget that you are two individuals and never let the "I" in you overrule the "you" of the other.'

Father Terry became a friend. He was also the first Catholic priest I got to know. And he's the only genuine man of God I have ever met. So when I encounter others of the cloth, I judge them by his standards. They always fall short.

Looking back—to be honest, I wasn't even aware of this at the time—our marriage was a success because Nisha was able to discern that I was both an adult and a child. I believe she loved both halves of me, although the child did occasionally grate on her nerves.

Perhaps this is why she often called me 'KT Baba'. In return I called her 'Waffles'.

Whenever Nisha travelled out of London on work—and that could happen for as many as seven or ten days a month—she would arrange for one of our close friends to 'babysit' me. However, each time she would add an admonition: 'You've got to learn to spend an evening on your own, without fretting or feeling miserable.' I never did.

I'd like to believe that our marriage brought Nisha luck. When I first met her, she was an investment banker with JP Morgan. Within a year, her career accelerated with rocket-like speed. After a succession of moves that took her to Manufacturers Hanover Trust Company and Merrill Lynch, she ended up as an executive director at County NatWest. By the age of thirty, she was widely recognized as one of the few high-flying female investment bankers in the City, London's financial centre.

Although by then I was a producer at London Weekend Television (LWT) and, in comparison to other journalists, well paid, Nisha's salary was almost seven times more than mine. One of her perks was a ridiculously low mortgage, which allowed us to buy a spacious and beautiful flat in St James's Gardens in Holland Park for over 100,000 pounds before either of us had reached our thirtieth birthday.

Nisha was never flashy but she was always conscious that she earned more than me and worried this might give me a complex. So whenever we went shopping and I would admire a jacket or a pair of shoes or an objet d'art in a shop window, she'd immediately say, 'I'll buy it for you.' It was Nisha's way of indicating that her money was also mine.

Nisha was a great organizer. Not only did she have a clear idea of the career path she intended for herself, she was also extremely good at identifying people who could be of use to me. And if I was too shy to approach them, she would go forth and do it herself.

By 1989 it seemed Nisha was destined to reach the top of her profession. Although already close to the summit, her colleagues were convinced that the last few hurdles would soon be crossed, possibly within a decade. The gods were clearly smiling on us.

Nisha's sudden death was, therefore, a devastating blow. She fell ill during an Easter break in Istanbul and it was quickly diagnosed as encephalitis. It happened on Easter Saturday in a city where English was not easily understood and where we knew absolutely no one. That only added to the trauma.

Ironically, encephalitis was something Nisha was familiar with. A few weeks earlier, Praveen's brother Deepak had been diagnosed with it in Bombay. As a neurologist who knew more about the disease than most doctors, Praveen had flown back to India to supervise Deepak's treatment. Nisha would call him every day to enquire about Deepak. Thus, encephalitis became a central topic of concern for her, Praveen's newly married wife Uma, and me.

It was, therefore, an unbelievable coincidence that Nisha should contract the same disease. When the doctors at the American Hospital in Istanbul told me that this was what they suspected, I knew I had to get her back to London and admitted to the National Hospital, where Praveen worked. But Nisha was in a coma and London is shut over Easter. Fortunately, I found her managing director Philip Porter's number in her diary and rang him up. Within hours, an ambulance plane flew in from Salzburg to take Nisha home.

Nisha lived for a month but never recovered. In fact, the coma got steadily worse. Meanwhile, Deepak died and Praveen returned to London without waiting for his brother's funeral obsequies. 'I wasn't able to save Deepak,' he told his father, 'but now I want to try and save Nisha. She is, after all, in my hospital.'

It wasn't to be. Two weeks later, the doctors declared her brainstem dead. Praveen's presence and confirmation of the verdict helped me accept it.

The advice from the National Hospital doctors was to switch off the machines. If Nisha could be said to be alive, it was only because the machines were keeping her going. Without their assistance she would not survive. This, they explained, was what brainstem death meant.

It was, however, a conversation with my father-in-law, Tony Meneses, who remained in India right through Nisha's illness, that encouraged me to accept the doctors' recommendation. In fact, it was the decisive factor.

'First,' he said, 'this is a decision for you to take on your own. Don't be swayed by what others tell you, whether it's my wife or your mother. But remember one thing as you make up your mind. So far, the doctors and nurses have given Nisha the best possible care because they believed she could survive. Now, when they're telling you she can't, if you insist on keeping her alive, won't their attitude change? Think about that.'

Till then, the pain of losing my wife had come in the way of viewing the situation from a detached perspective. My father-in-law, however, was gently pushing me in that direction. I heard him out in silence. I wasn't sure what to say. But he wasn't finished.

'Do you really want Nisha to become a vegetable?' It was a tough simile but I knew it was intended to force me to think clearly, not to hurt. 'Nisha's dignity is in your hands. Remember that only you can protect it and your decision will determine how others view her.'

The message from my father-in-law was obvious. *Let Nisha go,* was what he was saying. *Her life is over and you must not try to artificially extend it. That would diminish and demean her. It would be undignified.*

This also meant that I had to 'arrange' Nisha's death. A time had to be agreed upon when the machines would be switched off. Those most dear to Nisha had to be informed so they could be with her at that moment. I did what was required, almost mechanically but deliberately. At such times, this helps to keep one going. But was there something I was forgetting? I felt there was.

I instinctively knew I had the answer when I suddenly remembered Father Terry. He had been a friend since our wedding day. Although she wasn't religious, I felt Nisha would want him beside her. From the day we first met him, drinking his sherry while hiding our little secret, she had admired, respected and grown to like him.

I agreed to the hospital switching off the machines at 5 p.m. on Sunday, 22 April 1989. As the painful last hours and minutes ticked by, it was a sombre group that gathered around Nisha's hospital bed.

I won't say that Father Terry brought hope, but when he walked in at 4.30 p.m. he brought a sense of light. The gloom lifted, even if it did not dispel. Father Terry gave Nisha the last sacrament but also encouraged my mother to whisper Hindu prayers in her ear. Then he stood beside me as the machines slowly, painfully, flickered to a close and Nisha's life ebbed away.

Nisha and I had been married for six years, four months and nineteen days. We'd known each other for about two years prior to that. Now, at thirty-three—which also was her age when she died—I faced the rest of my life on my own.

5

STARTING A CAREER IN
TELEVISION

I can't deny that it was vanity that took me from *The Times* to London Weekend Television. I rather fancied the idea of seeing myself on screen.

When I returned to London in January 1982 after a winter vacation in Delhi—during which time I had learnt that the Nigerian government had withdrawn my accreditation—Charles Douglas-Home devised a series of challenging but horizon-expanding tasks to keep me occupied. One of these was a five-feature-article study of the Asian community in Britain.

'We need to get inside the community and find out what it thinks, how it views Britain, the problems it faces and the hopes it has,' Charlie explained. 'And as an Indian, surely you're the best person to do this for the paper?'

Prima facie what Charlie was saying made a lot of sense. But the truth was that the people who made up the Asian community in Britain—even those of Indian origin—came from a very different background and, consequently, had had very different life experiences to mine. We would actually be strangers to each other, even though we were all of Indian origin.

Charlie must have seen a flicker of doubt on my face because he suddenly laughed and said, 'Well, even if that isn't entirely true, it'll do you a lot of good to learn about your countrymen. This could be a sort of getting-to-know-India experience for you!'

It was. I spent two months in cities like Bradford, Wolverhampton, Birmingham, Manchester, Glasgow and, of course, the London suburb of Southall, which is where the Asian community resides in large, if not dominant, numbers. In Southall, I stayed as a paying guest after responding to an advertisement on a noticeboard in a popular eatery. It was a grubby home. Fortunately, I ate out, but I wore slippers even when I showered inside the tub!

In Manchester, I stayed with friends of friends. Elsewhere I stayed in bedsits or small inconspicuous hotels. In Bradford, I discovered a 'Crescent' where every house was occupied by Pathans. Back in Pakistan, they had all lived in the same village; now they had recreated a similar environment in this industrial town in Yorkshire.

My aim was to immerse myself into the South Asian community and try and become one of them whilst also learning about them. To belong but also observe, analyse and understand.

I think I must have been fairly successful because when *The Times* started publishing my articles, I received a call from LWT asking if I would be interested in working on a new television programme called *Eastern Eye*, which would be about the life, interests, concerns and celebrations of Britain's Asian community. This was to be one of LWT's offerings for Britain's new channel, Channel 4, due to be launched in the autumn of 1982.

As I've admitted, television appealed to me. It also paid a lot more. The only problem was that I would have to part company with Charlie, who had become more than a boss. He was by now a mentor.

When I told him, Charlie was all smiles. 'I knew this was going to happen one day,' he said. 'You're the sort who likes attention and grabs it when he can. Good for you. I'm sure you're doing the right thing.' There was a bit of a dig in the praise. Charlie knew how to deftly combine the two.

I accepted the offer from LWT as a bit of a lark. I approached it as an interesting experience. Little did I realize that I was embarking not just on a new job but a lifelong career. Practically everything I know about television—whether it's production or anchoring or scheduling—goes back to what I learnt, or taught myself, during the eight years I spent at London Weekend.

The 1970s and '80s were, arguably, the halcyon days of LWT. As a channel dedicated to weekend programming, it dominated the Independent Television (ITV) network schedule from Friday night to Monday morning. And because Saturdays and Sundays were when most people watched television, LWT had the biggest audiences. Consequently, its top anchors became household names across Britain. The list included David Frost, Janet Street-Porter, Peter Jay, Brian Walden, Auberon Waugh, Michael Aspel and Melvyn Bragg. Their programmes—*The 6 o'clock Show, The South Bank Show* and *Weekend World*, to name just three—were mandatory viewing for a lot of people.

When I joined, John Birt, who went on to become the director general of the British Broadcasting Corporation (BBC), was LWT's director of programmes. He was a shy and somewhat self-effacing man, yet it was said that no one knew more about the art of interviewing than he did.

Birt famously believed that there were only four answers to any question an interviewer might ask—yes, no, don't know, and won't tell. The job of the interviewer was to collapse the last two into the first two.

Birt also maintained that there were two types of interviews, the news interview and its current affairs half-brother. The first comprised a set of straightforward, obvious questions which, primarily, elicited information because one needed to know the details of what had happened. The bedrock of this type of interview was a quest to satisfy understandable curiosity.

The second interview, Birt argued, was very different. Here the aim was not to gather information, but to probe opinion or seek understanding and, thus, push the envelope further. This meant that the interviewer had to be a 'master' of the subject, in the sense that he or she must be aware of what were the possible answers and the costs connected to each of them. Finally, he or she had to explore what the solution might be and put that to the interviewee.

Such an interview, Birt maintained, was best done when the interviewee could be placed within the horns of a dilemma: damned if they do and damned if they don't. After establishing the interviewee's predicament, the first task of the interviewer was to push the guest to embrace one horn or the other. Once that was achieved, the next task was to point out the consequences of this choice and push the guest to accept or, at least, acknowledge them. The final task was to explore potential solutions to these costs and see which, if any, the interviewee was willing to endorse.

If an interviewer could push the ball thus far down the road, Birt believed that he would not just elicit a fairly comprehensive understanding of the issue he was exploring but, additionally, provide headline-making news for the next morning's papers. With this in mind, *Weekend World* was broadcast live every Sunday at noon. In the 1970s and early '80s, journalists across Britain would stop whatever they were doing to watch the show. Most major papers would lead on Monday with the scoop *Weekend World* had delivered the day before.

The highlight of my work on *Eastern Eye* were three interviews, but for reasons that had nothing to do with Birt. They were with the heads of government of Bangladesh, Pakistan and India, the three countries whose natives comprised Britain's Asian community. Each interview attracted attention and got talked about for rather odd reasons.

The interview with General Hussain Muhammad Ershad, then dictator of Bangladesh, became notorious for the way it ended. The general fancied himself as a poet and had composed a few special stanzas which he was determined to read out. With a solemn voice and a look suggesting that he had something important to say, his verse began: 'From the green fields of Bangladesh, bristling in the sun, to the good people of Britain, where there is none...'

I just about managed to keep a straight face, but it was sufficient to convince the dictator that I admired his poetry. He promised to send me more. Fortunately, either he forgot or his staff ensured it never reached me.

The interview with Pakistan's General Zia-ul-Haq is memorable for what happened halfway through. We were, I think, quarrelling over Benazir Bhutto and whether in Zia's Pakistan she was free to say and do what she wanted to. His tense face was proof that this wasn't a line of questioning he was comfortable with. The tight smile on his face looked decidedly false.

Then suddenly from the porch outside the drawing room where the interview was being recorded, came a sound of car doors banging noisily. It's not the sort of thing you would expect when you're interviewing a military ruler. However, it completely changed the general's mood. Interrupting himself, he explained: 'That's my family coming home. You must meet them afterwards.' This seemed to relax him. He was a different man thereafter.

The interview wasn't broadcast live, but it was sent via satellite live to London and, thereafter, broadcast without editing. Thus, everyone heard this little interlude and it attracted as much attention as anything else the general had said.

For me, however, the memory that lingers is of the general's elaborate courtesy, though, to be honest, it was manufactured, even if artfully. When the interview ended, he escorted me to my car which by then was waiting in the front porch. After thanking him and bidding adieu, I got in and the car drove in a half-circle as it negotiated the round garden at the front of the house. When it was at the other end, with the porch at the back, Gen. Zia's aide-de-camp (ADC) suddenly said: 'Look back, Mr Thapar, the general is waving.'

I turned to discover Gen. Zia standing exactly where he had shaken my hand and bid goodbye. Now, however, he was waving at the departing car. Clearly, this was a practice the general had made a habit of. What's more, his ADC was aware of this, which is why, even when we had our backs to the general, he was able to alert me. No other interviewee, either then or in the decades to follow, has used courtesy so deliberately to create a favourable impression.

The third interview, this time with Rajiv Gandhi, became famous because of what it revealed about him. For a start, the audience fell in love with his dimples and engaging smile. Though articulate, he had a shy manner that was endearing. But it was his language that caught everyone's attention. It was informal and quite un-prime ministerial. I don't remember what my question was, but this was the answer that won all-round praise: 'You don't expect me to tell you on telly, do you?'

There was also a fourth interview with a memorable story, though it happened entirely off-camera. This one was with P.V. Narasimha Rao, then union home minister. It took place in January 1985, weeks after Indira Gandhi's assassination and Rajiv Gandhi's notorious defence of the Sikh massacre that followed on the grounds that 'when a big tree falls, the earth will shake'. In one of his answers, Narasimha Rao said something similar. I noticed, but let it pass. This was a ten-minute interview and I needed to move on to other issues rather than spend time pursuing an indiscreet response. But unknown to me, Narasimha Rao was clearly disturbed by what he considered a damaging lapse.

The interview over, I returned to the hotel and was taking a shower when the phone rang. I reached out from behind the curtain to take the call. The voice on the other end claimed to be Narasimha Rao.

'Sure,' I snapped. 'And I'm Rajiv Gandhi. Now stop it, Siddo, and let me have a shower.' This was precisely the sort of prank my nephew, Siddo Deva, would frequently play.

'No, Karan, this really is Narasimha Rao, the home minister.'

'I'm sorry, minister. I thought you were my nephew trying to make a fool of me. What's happened?'

Narasimha Rao explained that he was worried about something he had said in the interview. He believed it could inflame opinions in India which, under the circumstances at the time, was not just undesirable but could be particularly damaging. Would LWT drop that answer?

I told the minister that the interview had already been sent through satellite to London and I would have to ask my bosses if they were willing to make the cut. I wasn't sure whether the answer would be yes.

'Please try your best,' he requested. I promised I would.

When I rang up LWT, I discovered that this was a matter that had to be referred all the way to the top. So it wasn't a short or simple phone call. Eventually, when it ended up in John Birt's hands, the answer I received was a delight.

'Tell Mr Rao that we make a career stitching up ministers,' Birt began. 'Now, for a change, it will be a pleasure to unstitch one instead.'

Narasimha Rao got the joke at once. I could tell he was laughing, even though I couldn't hear the sound over the phone. 'Tell Mr Birt I'm grateful and I like his sense of humour.'

After three years on *Eastern Eye*, I was appointed a producer on *Weekend World*, one of LWT's most highly regarded current affairs programmes. The three years I spent on *Weekend World* and the fourth on its successor programme *The Walden Interview* probably marked the steepest learning curve in my career as a journalist. The rigorous manner in which *Weekend World* approached the subjects it discussed taught me two things that have proved invaluable thereafter.

First, I learnt to think in a clear, linear fashion. 'Push your thought to the furthest extreme it takes you' was the accepted mantra of the programme. When you did, you could come to surprising but still logical conclusions.

The second lesson was how to structure a story. The idea was not to discount or ignore elements that were difficult to accommodate in the line you had adopted, but to find a way of incorporating them without damaging the logic of your argument. In part this was a writing technique, but more often, it required going back to the starting point and thinking your way through the issue all over again. Never easy, but always rewarding if you did it rigorously.

This meant that *Weekend World* documentaries were very different to those made by competing BBC programmes like *Panorama*. We would think our way through the story and carefully structure a script before starting to shoot. Consequently, we knew fairly precisely what we were looking for. Others tended to shoot first and then script according to the footage they had obtained. As a result, *Weekend World* was more cerebral but less visual. Its strength was its focus and penetrating direction. *Panorama*, on the other hand, was more beautiful to watch, full of delightful human touches, which were revealing and emotionally gripping. But the actual logic and structure could often be all over the place. Intellectually, *Panorama* often felt messy.

When I started working on *Weekend World*, Brian Walden, the anchor, was at the peak of his fame. A favourite of Margaret Thatcher—or so it was said—she gave some of her most famous interviews to him. Indeed, it was Brian who dubbed her social philosophy 'Victorian values'. Mrs Thatcher loved the term and readily agreed. After all, dedication, persistence, thrift and a black-and-white idea of right and wrong were values close to her heart.

I first met Margaret Thatcher in 1975, while I was still at Cambridge. At the time she was the upstart leader of the opposition, dismissed by Tory grandees as a mere Grantham grocer's daughter. Dressed in a bright canary-yellow dress trimmed with a startling black band, she was hard to miss. Her voice was also rasping. The refined faux-upper-class accent was still years away. Consequently, she caught one's attention but did not necessarily win one's admiration.

Maggie Thatcher had come to the Cambridge Union as a special speaker. The university mood was dominated by the belief that Prime Minister James Callaghan's Lib–Lab Pact of 1977–78 (between the Liberal Democrats and the Labour Party) could deliver. The winter of discontent was three years ahead. At the time, the avuncular prime minister was both liked and trusted.

Impressions changed dramatically when Thatcher started to speak. There was something about her delivery that forced you to listen. There was a lot more to her content that made you sit up and think. But above all, her passion and conviction stole the day. It was years before her economics won widespread support, but the feeling that she could make it to the top and even dominate British politics had already begun to rouse emotions, both in favour and against.

I was a member of the Cambridge Union's Standing Committee and got to meet Mrs Thatcher over coffee and sandwiches. Perhaps I was overawed by her manner or lost in reverie, but I recall her repeating a polite question I had failed to answer. It was a casual enquiry about what I was studying and when I replied 'political philosophy', she harrumphed. 'Rather you than me,' she snorted. 'I prefer to get on with things!'

The next time we met, she was prime minister and had just won her third successive election. The coiffed hair, large pearl earrings and carefully, if artificially, modulated voice were firmly in place. She was, after all, at the crest of her political power. Her position was unchallenged.

I was part of a team from LWT at 10 Downing Street to record an interview. Afterwards, she invited us to stay for a beer and then, jug in hand, circulated around the room, topping up glasses.

As she did the rounds, Mrs Thatcher filled the glass of a new redhead Cockney spark who, brimming with enthusiasm, burst into eager conversation.

'Ma'am,' he began, addressing her as if she was the queen, 'there's a question I have to ask.'

'Well,' Mrs Thatcher replied, unruffled by the surprise elevation. 'Go ahead.'

'When do you agree to give an interview and when do you refuse?'

The prime minister froze. Clearly, this was not what she had expected. But the question posed a challenge and she wasn't going to duck it.

'When I'm in trouble, when things are going wrong and when my stock is falling, I say yes.' Then she paused for effect. 'But when it's smooth sailing I prefer to keep silent.'

'Shouldn't it be the other way round?' The redhead thought he had detected an anomaly and wasn't ready to let it pass.

Mrs Thatcher laughed. It sounded forced. She was never good at allowing her emotions to show.

'When things seem to be collapsing, I need to prove I'm in charge and that I have the answers. I also need to reassure people. That's the time to speak out. But if you do so when the going is good, chances are you'll put your foot in your mouth and fall over your own feet. At such times it's better to keep mum.'

How true. Unfortunately, in India, our politicians do the opposite. They choose to crow whenever they can and thus invite misfortune. But when they need to bolster public confidence, reassure supporters and silence critics, they're as quiet as church mice. Actually, that poor animal scurries around and is at least noticed. Not our politicians. When in trouble, they become invisible.

∾

'You media guys are the cause of at least half the so-called political dissidence we read about,' Arun Jaitley once sagely commented, although I suspect he may no longer remember when or why he made this observation. It may even have been said jocularly, but then many a truth is spoken in jest.

Arun's remark reminds me of something Mrs Thatcher once said of Norman St John-Stevas. He was, briefly, a colourful if inconsequential member of her Cabinet. His reputation was built on his differences with her. He christened her 'the blessed Margaret', a tongue-in-cheek reference to her saint-like rectitude but also her unbending obstinacy. The British don't like saints. They distrust them.

'Speaking of Norman,' said Mrs Thatcher in one of her interviews to Sir Robin Day, the premier television interrogator of his time, 'he had no idea he was a major dissident until he read of it in the papers and then belatedly started to behave like one.'

Whether her sarcasm was an accurate reflection on the role of the press might be debatable, but it was certainly sufficient to finish off poor Norman. He retired to the House of Lords and well-deserved obscurity.

The point Arun and Lady Thatcher (as she subsequently became) wanted to make was uncannily similar. There is something about the way newspapers and television report differences of political opinion that converts them into seeming dissidence. Perhaps it's their narrow focus, or the exaggerated attention, or even the suggested opposition in views that does it. Or maybe it's inherent in the very nature of political reportage. Disagreements don't matter unless they are significant. And if they are significant, surely they must be more than differences of opinion? This logic may be circular but it's also unquestionable.

So are journalists guilty—if that's the word—of making honest and straightforward differences seem like disagreements and dissidence? And if we are, is that tantamount to manufacturing what we then report and comment on? Or do politicians, perhaps understandably and at times even cleverly, blame journalists for the problems they cannot reconcile or resolve?

Perhaps it's a bit of all these. Donald Trump would, of course, call it fake news!

∽

It was during my time at LWT that I also started writing leaders, or lead articles, for *The Times*. To be honest, I was somewhat taken aback when Charlie suggested this. 'I've never written a leader in my life,' I said.

Charlie laughed. By now I knew this would be his instinctive response to many of my questions. 'I know, but then you'd never written an article when you first started with *The Times*. You're the sort of chap who likes being thrown into the deep end because you know how to swim. You'll get the hang of it pretty soon.'

My initial remit covered the countries of the subcontinent: India, Pakistan, Bangladesh, Nepal and Sri Lanka. However, it soon expanded to include the Maldives and, occasionally, Afghanistan. I knew some of these countries well, but there were others where my knowledge was limited. In the early years, one such was Pakistan.

This was the Zia decade, when momentous developments could happen without warning. When they did, I would reach out to Maleeha Lodhi for help. Today she's better known for her two stints as Pakistan's ambassador in America, a spell as high commissioner in the UK and her present tenure as the country's permanent representative at the United Nations. But in those days she was simply teaching at the London School of Economics.

Few people I know have the encyclopaedic knowledge she carries in her head. No matter what the subject, she always had the details of its background. More importantly, she could also swiftly analyse the likely consequences that might follow most developments.

So whenever *The Times* rang for a leader on something that had just happened in Pakistan, I'd pick up the phone and ring Maleeha. Often we would meet for a quick lunch but sometimes if she was busy, she'd explain on the phone. She was always ready to help.

Looking back on the leaders I wrote, they were analytical rather than prescriptive. From my perch in London, my understanding of the subjects I tackled was sufficient to suggest knowledge and insight without overwhelming the readership with confusing detail. My London-based perspective made it easier to explain subcontinental issues to a British or international readership. Perhaps Indians or Pakistanis or Bangladeshis would have found the leaders somewhat general, but they were not really meant for them.

There was one occasion when I did get into trouble. During my visit to Pakistan to interview Gen. Zia, I filed a leader on his constitutional amendments. While pointing out the many ways in which these were undemocratic, I also claimed that they did not permit the president to be removed from office.

A few days after its publication, by when I was back in London, the Pakistan high commissioner called up Charlie and asked to meet him. Charlie sensed it had to do with the leader and suggested that I should be present.

'Do you really think that's a good idea?' I asked.

'Why?' Charlie sounded perplexed.

'Once the high commissioner sees me, he'll know that your leaders on Pakistan are written by an Indian. Given the relationship between the two countries, is it wise you should let this cat out of the bag?'

Charlie got the point at once. 'You're probably right. I'll see him on my own and let you know what he has to say.'

So the next day, after the high commissioner had met him, I got a call from Charlie. As usual, he started with a laugh.

'He really is a silly little man,' Charlie said. 'He's annoyed by the point made in your leader that the president can't be removed. Apparently, if 98 per cent of the people vote to do so, he can be turfed out. So technically, we were wrong.'

My heart sank. I'd made a factual error that should never have happened and, as a result, I had embarrassed *The Times*. I immediately apologized and asked Charlie what he proposed to do.

'The silly little man insisted on an apology, so I had to agree. But don't worry—we'll write it in small print and bury it somewhere at the back of the paper!'

That is precisely what happened the next day. So well was it hidden, it took me a while to find the apology!

Charlie never held this episode against me. It didn't alter his confidence in me. Consequently, this was the best lesson I learnt about how a boss can support his colleagues and win their loyalty forever.

Writing leaders never conflicted with my responsibilities at LWT. Once I got the hang of it, they could easily be done either late at night or during a slow spell in the afternoon. But there were two interviews I did for *The Times* which clearly amounted to cheating on LWT. At the time, I placated my conscience with the specious argument that they had been done on the phone and not recorded on camera, and that LWT would probably not have been interested in these interviews anyway.

The first was with Benazir Bhutto on the day Gen. Zia died in a plane crash. His sudden removal meant that elections had to be called and she was the most likely winner.

So, hours after the general's death, when I phoned Benazir, she was happy to grant an interview, though it had to be done hurriedly. She was now at the centre of a sudden swirl of developments and desperately short of time.

I managed to talk for about twenty-five minutes. To this, I added excerpts of earlier interviews, including one while she had been in London, where she'd talked about how she would handle power if she ever became prime minister.

The interview was published on the op-ed page of *The Times* the following day and it made a splash. Unfortunately, this meant that practically everyone at LWT got to see it. They now knew why I had suddenly been absent after lunch the previous day. No one told me off but I could sense the disapproval.

The second interview was even more fortuitous. It was with Aung San Suu Kyi. More importantly, it happened just days after she'd been put under house arrest.

I told *The Times* that she was an old friend and I was confident that if I could get through, she'd give me an interview. So, once again, I quietly disappeared from LWT and placed myself in a quiet room at *The Times*. The paper's office was at Wapping, a remote and rarely visited corner of London, and no one was likely to discover I was there.

It was Michael Aris, Suu's husband, who picked up the phone when I got through to Rangoon (Yangon). 'How on earth did you manage?' he asked. 'This phone is supposed to have been cut off.'

Yet it was a perfect line. Normally, the connection was full of crackle and it would be difficult to make out what was being said. On this occasion, it felt as if I was talking to someone in the next room.

After a minute, Michael said, 'Would you like to speak to Suu? She's here beside me.'

It had been a couple of years since I had last met Suu. During that period her mother, who used to pamper me as a child when she was the Burmese ambassador in India in the early 1960s, had died. As a result, I forgot why I'd called and began talking about the past.

'Have you just rung for a chat?' Suu suddenly interrupted. 'Don't you want to do an interview before the authorities realize what has happened and cut this line? This could be your only opportunity.'

Only then did the interview get underway. I had already wasted five minutes chatting aimlessly. Luckily, the line stayed intact and I was able to ask all the questions I wanted. In fact, there were a few times when Michael took the phone and added a couple of sentences to complete an answer he thought Suu had needlessly abbreviated.

I'm not sure how long it took the Burmese junta to discover that Suu's phone was working, but the interview this inexplicably functioning phone line permitted attracted considerable attention when it was published by *The Times* the next day. Years later, when Suu published her book, *Freedom from Fear,* the full transcript was part of it. Obviously, she was as pleased with the outcome as I was. And this time LWT didn't seem displeased. Or, at least, I couldn't sense it.

∾

I thought I was firmly settled at LWT and likely to spend a lifetime there when fate suddenly and dramatically intervened. Nisha died. It didn't take me long to realize that this had changed everything.

Because of her stellar career, we had decided to put off having children till Nisha was thirty-six, an age beyond which she felt it would be unwise to wait. At that point, Nisha also thought, we would need to take a decision—either to return home and bring up our children in an Indian environment or commit ourselves to Britain forever and ensure they fully belong to that country.

Now that Nisha had died at thirty-three, I realized that the decision to return to India or remain in Britain had to be taken immediately. Her death meant that I had to rebuild my life and it was necessary to decide where I would do so.

I opted for India, thus bringing to an end nine years with LWT. However, the skills I took to Delhi were a direct product of this experience. In India, I concentrated on interviews and discussions, but if they seemed different to what other anchors were doing, it was because I consciously applied the lessons I had learnt in London. The imprimatur of LWT was there for all to see.

6

BENAZIR BECOMES A CLOSE FRIEND

It was during her years of self-exile in London that my university friendship with Benazir Bhutto matured into a stronger and closer bond. This was helped by the fact that I was married by then, and Benazir and Nisha grew to like and understand each other.

To begin with, of course, Benazir was a journalistic catch. As the de facto leader of Pakistan's battered democracy—not to mention that she was also the principal opponent to Gen. Zia—Benazir was inevitably courted by *Eastern Eye*. She would enhance our ratings, while we could offer her the perfect platform to reach out to both the Asian community in Britain and Pakistanis at home.

One of the first things I did after her arrival in London was to invite her to lunch. It was held at the formal dining room in the London Weekend office, around a table set with a white linen tablecloth and napkins, silver candelabra and cutlery, and hallmarked china crockery. This only added to the intimidating effect Benazir had on my colleagues. Initially, at least, they were speechless. The other guests on the surrounding tables also seemed unable to take their eyes off her.

I had thought this would please Benazir, but I was wrong. Jail and adversity in Pakistan had tempered the person I used to know. Now she wanted to do more than just make a political impression. She wanted to get to know people and understand them. Their awe made that difficult, if not impossible.

'What about inviting me home?' she said when I dropped her back to her flat. 'I want to meet your wife and see your house.'

This was what I had been waiting for. I wasn't sure how much our relationship might have changed in the six years since we last met. Now, I knew that even though she had become a leading Pakistani politician in her own right and would soon be an international celebrity, she was still my old friend.

Benazir and Nisha took to each other almost immediately. With Nisha, Benazir would open up and talk about the personal tragedy her family had suffered, starting with her father's assassination, her separation from her two brothers and the continuing mistreatment by Gen. Zia. With me the discussion was initially more political. Between the two of us, Benazir found a home and friendship that allowed her to voice whatever issues were on her mind.

When her younger brother Shahnawaz died in the south of France, Benazir recounted the tragic story with tears running down her cheeks. For some reason we were sitting on the floor, drinking red wine while Nisha and Benazir smoked. In those days, Benazir still smoked occasionally. She was convinced that her Afghan sister-in-law had a role to play in Shahnawaz's death. She certainly had not been prompt to help or report his death.

Late at night and sometimes even in the wee hours of the morning, when it was time to leave, Benazir would ask me to call a cab. 'We've all drunk too much and you're not going to drive me home,' she would laugh and say. 'Imagine what would happen if the police stop you and I'm found on the seat beside you.'

On the first such occasion when the taxi driver turned out to be South Asian, I discovered another side of her complex and self-protective personality. Benazir kissed Nisha's cheeks but pointedly held out her hand when it was time to bid me goodbye. This took me aback because till then, she had never hesitated to put her cheek forward.

'Careful, careful,' she whispered. 'He's from our part of the world. He mustn't see you kissing me. Remember, I'm an unmarried woman from a Muslim country.'

That was, of course, well known but its implication and how that, in turn, would put a clamp on her behaviour had never occurred to me. For Benazir, however, always conscious of the fact that her future lay in politics in Pakistan, this was a key concern.

Over the next few years we met fairly regularly. Occasionally, Nisha and I would take her out to dinner. But more often she preferred to come home, put her feet up and chat into the late hours, sipping wine and sometimes smoking. So it was a surprise when she called up one day in 1985 and said, 'I need to discuss something with the two of you. When can I come over?'

Benazir had decided to return to Pakistan. She had realized that she couldn't put off doing so for much longer. Exile in London was diminishing the contact she valued with her people. But more than that, I suspect, there was the challenge to prove that she could take on a dictator and get Pakistan to support her the way the people had stood by her father in the 1960s, when he had taken on Field Marshal Ayub Khan who was the military dictator at the time. Benazir knew that she had to confront a similar challenge and win.

Actually, she didn't need our support or advice. Her mind was made up. She was a resolute person who always knew what she wanted to do. But she felt the need to personally tell us. That was important for her. It was one of the little things that reflected her personal warmth.

I dropped in to say goodbye on her last night and, not surprisingly, she was surrounded by supporters, friends, advisers and hangers-on. Each room in her small flat was packed. 'Wish me luck, wish me luck,' she said. I noticed that her fingers were crossed. But she was smiling. Now that she had made up her mind and was returning the next day, she looked radiant. Somewhere inside, she knew that destiny was calling.

Benazir took Pakistan by storm and today, when you look back on that incredible return, it seems inevitable. But at the time it was very different. Under her confident exterior she was apprehensive. That was why she had planned her return meticulously.

Benazir chose to fly home via Saudi Arabia. She did this for two reasons. First, she wanted to pay her respects at Mecca. Equally importantly, she wanted to land in Lahore rather than Karachi. And in those days the only international flight to Lahore was Saudia (Saudi Arabian Airlines) from Riyadh.

The reason Lahore was so important wasn't immediately clear to me. 'I have to make a mark in Punjab to prove to the country that I have popular support,' Benazir explained. 'Arriving first in Karachi won't be the same thing. No matter how many turn out to meet me, it will always be said that this is local Sindhi support. Punjab is the heart of Pakistan and that's where I must begin.'

When we met after her return home, Benazir told me how difficult the flight from Riyadh to Lahore had been. She was in first class and almost entirely alone; the rest of her entourage was at the back of the plane. As it flew through the clouds she stared out of the window, wondering what sort of reception she would get. She knew her future depended on it.

When the plane landed, Benazir said that she kept peering out of the window only to find the airport silent and deserted. This didn't feel like a rapturous welcome. Her heart began to sink. 'Is my political career over before it's even started?' was the question she kept asking herself.

There were three people at the bottom as she climbed down the stairs. Beyond them stretched empty space and an eerie silence. It was shortly after dawn, but there seemed to be no signs of life at the airport.

'Bibijaan,' one of the three said to her, 'the authorities have not allowed anyone to enter the airport but there are millions outside waiting for you.'

It took Benazir eighteen hours to drive from the airport to the Minar-e-Pakistan in the centre of Lahore, a journey that should have taken no more than half an hour. It seemed as if the whole city—perhaps even the entire province—was out on the streets to welcome her home.

In the weeks that followed, such displays of mass support for Benazir were repeated in Quetta, Islamabad and Karachi. By then it was clear that Gen. Zia's nemesis had arrived and captured the love and support of the Pakistani people. The clock of his departure was now steadily ticking and growing louder with every chime.

About a year after her return, I made a trip to Islamabad to interview Gen. Zia's prime minister, Muhammad Khan Junejo, but ensured that I returned to London via Karachi. That gave me a few hours to meet Benazir. She tried to persuade me to accompany her the next morning to Larkana, the Bhutto ancestral home in the interior of Sindh. I told her that my visa didn't permit me to leave Karachi city perimeters.

'Oh, don't worry about that.' She laughed. 'We'll smuggle you out and no one will know.' Hameed Haroon, then the young publisher of *The Dawn*, was at her home that evening and promised to accompany me if I agreed to go. Unfortunately, I'm not cut out for such thrills and insisted on returning safely to London. 'Coward' was Benazir's verdict. She was right.

When she was getting married to Asif Zardari, Benazir rang up to ask if Nisha and I would come. Nisha couldn't, but I stopped in Karachi on my way back for a Christmas vacation in Delhi.

Karachi was agog with anticipation. In fact, most of Pakistan was. Taxi drivers were calling it the wedding of the century and the city's hotels were filled to capacity. 'Congratulations to the daughter of Pakistan from the people of Pakistan,' proclaimed the welcoming banner at the airport as guests began to arrive. Convoys of buses with the Pakistan Peoples Party (PPP) flag aloft, gaily dressed women packed inside and strains of the shehnai competing with noisy exhausts raced through the streets.

On the day before the wedding, schoolgirls danced and sang outside the bridal house, heralding the mehndi ceremony, the most important prenuptial ritual. Traditionally, this should have been a 'ladies only' event, as the cream-red-and-gold invitations maintained. But it ended up a combined evening with several of Asif's friends joining in. Benazir's sahelis got it off to a rollicking start, singing tapas, Sindhi and Baluch geets and teasing Asif.

'*Asif-ji, Asif-ji, honewale jijaji,*' they jibed. '*Shaadi ke saat phere hain aur hamari saat sharte hain.*' (Asif-ji, Asif-ji, brother-in-law-to-be, you have to fulfil seven of our conditions). He readily agreed to each of them, and then joined them on the floor. As he danced, they finally clapped, symbolically accepting the marriage.

The wedding on Friday, 18 December 1987, had several thousands wonderstruck, the city at a standstill, and everyone gossiping and swapping stories till late into the night. It was an evening of massive numbers, glittering jewellery and almost unstoppable jubilation. The nikaah ceremony, held exclusively for friends and relatives in the gardens of the Bhutto family home at 70 Clifton, was the beginning. Benazir emerged radiant in a parrot-green and shocking-pink lehenga with matching emeralds and rubies. Asif was in a cream silk salwar-kameez, a Sindhi patka turban and a silk shawl to match his bride's colours. But at the start of the ceremony he was nowhere to be seen.

With family members exuberantly ululating in the background, the bride—seated on an elegant mandap, wreathed in strings of jasmines and scarlet roses, and covered by a thin pale-pink veil—signed her marriage contract. Almost everyone noted the time: it was just before five minutes to 6. The rites accompanying the marriage ceremony were based on Iranian customs, the country where Benazir's mother Nusrat Bhutto was said to come from.

The simple ceremony consisted of a family 'qazi' asking Benazir on three separate occasions if she consented to Asif's proposal. After her third assent, she signed the contract. Then, escorted from inside the house by his sisters and cousins, Asif joined Benazir on the dais. They sat together, covered by her pink veil and a gleaming mirror was held under it so they could see each other. Finally, following Sindhi custom, first Asif's mother, then Benazir's aunt, touched the couple's heads together thrice to wish them luck and happiness.

The scene then shifted to the neighbouring Clifton Gardens as the privileged guests made their way through the thousands of friendly onlookers and the Karachi crowd gathered outside for the larger reception. Here, over 1,500 more guests had turned up, dripping in jewels, clad in colourful silks, swept up by the excitement of the occasion. When the newly married Zardaris arrived to take their place on a specially crafted bigger stage, the guests surrounded them in an uncontrolled desire to see, touch and greet the couple.

As the grande dames of Karachi society jumped onto the stage, with their husbands struggling not far behind, parts of the floor sagged. For a time, the numbers, the stampede of photographers and the reflex action of desperate security men suggested an impending tragedy. It was averted—dinner was served and the food diverted the crush.

Benazir had changed for this second stage. She now wore a striking white-and-gold salwar-kameez, set off by sparkling sapphires and diamonds. The guests fought and struggled to get close to the glowing bride.

But the high point of the evening was the public reception held for the 'ordinary people of Karachi', as they were then called, in the vast Kakri grounds. The entire square, once a football ground, was gaily decked out with coloured lights and huge posters of the Bhuttos, both father and daughter. Kakri has a special significance for the Bhuttos. It was here that Zulfikar Ali Bhutto made his last public speech before the 1977 coup. A year before the wedding, Benazir had been arrested while addressing a rally at this site.

At a guesstimate, two lakh people had gathered to greet the newly-weds. The couple came to the venue shortly before 10 p.m. to sit on a raised platform surrounded by friends and relatives. Singers and dancers entertained and a display of colourful fireworks went on till late into the night.

It was more than a wedding; more than a celebration. It was like a festival, part private, part political, but at all times spontaneous. There were moments when the arrangements collapsed due to the excitement and the impatience. Processions of Benazir's supporters, organized by her Pakistan Peoples Party, danced on the streets. Many hung out of cars waving the party flag and blasting songs composed in her honour. Some even fired shots in the air, in typical Sindhi feudal tradition. One of these shots accidentally killed a woman at the Kakri grounds celebration before the married couple arrived. Elsewhere, eight people who had climbed up a tree got injured when the branch snapped, sending their machan tumbling down.

I only saw Benazir briefly at the wedding itself. Not surprisingly, we hardly got to chat. But early the next morning, she called to say that she had asked a friend to bring me over for dinner. 'You have to cancel whatever you're doing, otherwise what was the point of coming to Karachi?'

Dinner was at her in-laws' home, where Benazir and Asif had been given a small cottage in the garden. It was just the two of them, her friend and me. It was also the first time I got to properly meet and talk to Asif.

The first thing that struck me about him was his playful teasing. He kept pulling Benazir's leg. No one else in Pakistan could take this liberty. But Benazir clearly liked it. She giggled each time Asif called her 'the great one'.

Asif's humour was in many ways his greatest asset. Referring to Benazir's 'battalion of sahelis', he laughed and said: 'I've told them they can visit us once a week. Beyond that, I've told the guards to keep the gates shut! But when it comes to Benazir, I think she may be the one to discipline me.'

I instinctively felt that this was a good way of bringing a measure of balance into Benazir's life. Otherwise, the adulation of the crowds and the fawning of her supporters would place her on a pedestal and put her beyond human reach.

In the years that followed, Benazir was twice elected prime minister of Pakistan. This made her a person I was repeatedly keen to interview. But it also created a unique problem. She was a politician who knew things she did not wish to reveal. I was a journalist anxious to ferret out what she did not want to say. That made for an inevitable conflict of interest.

What made matters worse was that she always thought she was giving an interview to a friend. On the other hand, I was determined to prove that friendship would not weaken or undermine my journalistic principles. This added to the tension that underlay our interviews.

Now, Benazir loved ice cream. She could eat vast quantities of it. In later years, her favourite became Ben & Jerry's. Whenever I finished a particularly acrimonious interview, she would insist that we eat ice cream together. 'It will cool you down!' she would joke.

There were several interviews we did that annoyed her, a few that upset her and at least one that riled her. But she never held that against me. She accepted that a journalist had a job to do, just as she insisted that a politician couldn't answer every question. She always ensured that our professional relationship—as interviewer and prime minister or opposition leader—remained separate from our friendship.

As a young politician, in the years after her father's cruel hanging, she had often consciously modelled herself on Indira Gandhi. I remember her fascination for the traditional Indian namaste. 'It's dignified, friendly but not familiar,' she once said. I suspect the adab that she made her personal greeting was, in her eyes, an equivalent.

In 1984, when Maqbool Butt was about to be hanged, Benazir wrote to Indira Gandhi, pleading he be saved. 'Why are you doing that?' I asked. I couldn't understand her need to write the letter. I thought it was a mistake.

'I have to, Karan,' she explained. 'I've lived through my father's hanging and I know the trauma it created for the family. I can't watch someone else go through the same misery without doing what I can to prevent it.'

Indira Gandhi never replied but Benazir didn't hold that against her.

As a Bhutto daughter, Benazir was always conscious of her family's similarity with the Gandhis. After Sanjay Gandhi's plane crash and Indira's assassination in the early 1980s were followed by her brother Shahnawaz's mysterious death, she once commented that there was a curse on both families. At the time, Rajiv's killing and her own were still far in the future. Today, there can be no doubt about that curse.

In 1988, when Rajiv visited Islamabad during the early weeks of her first prime ministership, she invited him and Sonia to a private family dinner on their first night there. Her husband Asif, mother Nusrat and sister Sanam were the only other people present. In those days, a common joke in both countries was that Rajiv and Benazir should marry each other and sort out their two countries' problems. Benazir told me that they laughed over this at dinner.

'Rajeev'—as she always pronounced his name, adopting a Punjabi accent which was clearly misplaced in a Westernized Sindhi—'is so handsome,' she said when I next met her. And then she added, 'But he's equally tough.'

During the Bharatiya Janata Party (BJP) years, Benazir forged a link with the Advani family with the same facility and friendship as with Rajiv. A few months after her first meeting with L.K. Advani, we were together in Washington for the annual National Prayer Breakfast in 2002. During a break in one of the sessions, she insisted that I accompany her for shopping. 'But we're walking, okay? I need the exercise and so do you!'

As we sauntered down Connecticut Avenue, she stopped outside an old-fashioned bookshop. Minutes later, she bought a Robert Kaplan paperback as a gift for Advani. I carried it back to Delhi. It was the first of several similar gifts she sent him.

I know that as prime minister, her two terms in office disillusioned many. Her fans were disappointed while her critics felt justified. But between 1989 and 2007, the change that characterized her attitude towards India, and Kashmir, in particular, progressed steadily and didn't falter. From the young prime minister who would shout 'Azadi, Azadi, Azadi!' on television, she became the first, the most consistent and perhaps the strongest proponent of a joint India–Pakistan solution to Kashmir. As early as 2001, she began to speak about soft borders, free trade and even, perhaps unrealistically, a joint Parliament for the two halves of Kashmir. General Pervez Musharraf's concept of self-governance and joint management drew heavily upon her thinking.

When I last interviewed her in September 2007, days before her return to Pakistan, she went further than ever before. Not only did she forcefully repeat her commitment to clamp down on all private militia and shut terrorist camps but, in addition, she promised to consider the extradition of Dawood Ibrahim and even the possibility of giving India access to men like Lashkar-e-Taiba supremo Hafiz Muhammad Saeed and Jaish-e-Mohammad founder Masood Azhar.

In private conversations, she would readily admit that the strident prime minister persona of 1988–89 was a mistake. In fact, once she even came close to saying as much on television. Had she lived to become prime minister for a third time, I feel certain she would have fulfilled her commitment to improve India–Pakistan relations.

Two months before her death, we met in Dubai. She was planning a second homecoming. When I asked if she could repeat the miracle of her first return, she shot back with the question, 'Why do you ask?' I told her that she was now fifty-four, had been prime minister twice, disappointed many and that Pakistan was a very different country these days.

She heard me out in silence and then softly smiled. Her eyes seemed to take on a knowing but playful look. When she spoke, her words sounded measured and well considered: 'It will be an even bigger return home.'

In fact, it was explosive. She was clearly poised for a huge victory. Sadly, death snatched it away. But I doubt whether Benazir would have wanted to die of old age. Instead, she died a hero, a martyr and an inspiration for many.

The day after her death, I received Benazir's new year's greeting card. It read: 'Praying for peace in the world and happiness for your family in 2008.' Unfortunately, both were denied to her.

7

GETTING TO KNOW SANJAY GANDHI AND AUNG SAN SUU KYI

I can't claim that I was close to the entire Gandhi family, but there was a time when Sanjay, Indira Gandhi's younger son, was a good friend. In fact, he even tried to teach me to fly a plane, without success but with considerable daredevilry.

I first got to know Sanjay as my sister Shobha's friend. It was the early 1960s, Daddy was army chief and we were living in Army House on what was still called King George's Avenue (now Rajaji Marg) in Delhi. At the time, Sanjay was the prime minister's grandson and studying at St Columba's School. He was at least six years younger, but he developed a liking for Shobha that I suppose was calf-love.

Shobha was around twenty and Sanjay probably not more than fourteen. That age gap should have been an obstacle to any friendship, but it wasn't for him. Every afternoon after school, Sanjay would drop by to meet her. He wasn't particularly chatty and a lot of the time would simply sit in companionable silence. They would talk, play cards or listen to music. The rest of the family would be there as well. As afternoon turned to evening Indira Gandhi would ring to find out when he was coming home. She was worried that he hadn't done his homework. Mummy often had to reassure her that after an early supper, Sanjay would be sent back. This routine, however, seemed to repeat itself day after day.

After Shobha's marriage, Sanjay would turn up at her home in the evenings and spend hours chatting with her and her husband, Banjo. By then he was a young car mechanic building the prototype of his personally designed Maruti—which, years later, under different ownership and with a different design, came to dominate the Indian car market. He would drink countless cups of tea but there was no question of anything stronger. Even nimboo-pani seemed to be verboten. He was also a simple eater. In the early years of their marriage, when young couples are often penurious, dal-chawal was often all that Shobha could give him, but Sanjay ate it as if it was haute cuisine.

In contrast to his otherwise shy and quiet character, Sanjay was a daredevil. There was no challenge he would not accept. Once, on a warm winter afternoon, with the temperature in the comfortable twenties, my sisters insisted on being taken for a drive in his Jeep. They bullied him till he agreed. As we drove past Mehrauli, heading towards Chhatarpur, Shobha suddenly asked if he had the guts to drive up one of the hills on either side. She meant it as a taunt. He took it as a challenge.

Seconds later, he turned off the road and began driving uphill. The jeep started groaning but Sanjay kept changing gears to give it more power. Halfway up, it stalled. We were perched precariously and stationary upon a hillside. We could sense that the jeep would soon start slipping and sliding backwards. Panic began to overtake us. 'Get the hell out of here, Sanjay,' Shobha shouted. 'I was only joking, for Christ's sake.'

But Sanjay was made of sterner stuff. He was now enjoying this. The more precarious the situation seemed and the greater the fear, the bolder he seemed to become. Pushing the jeep into the four-wheel-drive mode and pressing the accelerator right to the floor, he drove on. But for every three feet we moved forward the jeep seemed to slide back one or two. By then everyone was screaming.

I'm not sure how it ended, but we got off the hill intact. Sanjay laughed all the way home. The rest of us sat ashen-faced and silent.

∾

The jump from being Shobha's kid brother to one of Sanjay's friends only happened in the mid-1970s. And it seemed to take place almost accidentally.

After Daddy's sudden death in 1975 two days before the Emergency was declared—he died of a heart attack at the age of sixty-nine—Sanjay started to drop in frequently. At first, Shobha was there but even after she left to go back to her own home in Moscow, where Banjo was posted with the embassy, Sanjay continued to visit. Mummy would ask him to fix door handles that had come undone or her transistor, which frequently gave trouble. For some reason that I never discovered, he would always sit on the floor, tackling the task he'd been given. But it was also the ideal opportunity for Sanjay and I to chat. That's how we got to know each other.

Over the next two years, whenever I was back on holiday, I saw a lot of him and his wife Maneka. As a result, I also got to meet Indira Gandhi. The most striking thing about her was how different her public persona was to the private individual. During the Emergency, many thought of her as a political monster but she was also a delightful personality. Sanjay was very protective of his mother and she clearly adored him.

74

The Indira Gandhi most people remember is the political virago who decimated the Syndicate, defeated Pakistan, stood up to America, appointed chief ministers at will, damaged institutions and imposed the Emergency. This was the forbidding side of her. It led Atal Bihari Vajpayee to call her 'Durga' and the Western media to label her 'The Empress of India'.

The private Indira Gandhi was surprisingly different. She was petite, with delicate, almost fragile hands. Her letters to Dorothy Norman reveal a troubled personality struggling between the political demands on her life and her inner wish for solitude and quiet contemplation.

Indira Gandhi also had an impish sense of fun. In the 1960s, when deference and formality still determined our lives, she organized a treasure hunt for one of Shobha's birthdays. The clues were innocently naughty. They included fish bones from Alps, a restaurant in Janpath, and a policeman's helmet. At the time, no one knew that the architect of this harmless mischief was Indira Gandhi. Even her two sons, who were at the party, had no idea of the clues their mother had devised.

In 1976, at the height of the Emergency when her power was unchallenged, I recall a breakfast at 1, Safdarjung Road before Indira Gandhi took my sisters and me to see one of the Pink Panther films at Rashtrapati Bhavan. When it was time for a quick pee before leaving for the cinema, my sister Premila asked her how she managed on her travels. I'll never forget her reply.

'It's a dreadful problem for every woman politician. Unlike men, we can't go behind a tree! So I drink all the water I need last thing at night in the hope that it's out of the system by the morning.'

Indira Gandhi also had a dry and subtle sense of humour. Once, while speaking to Peter Ustinov about the appalling state of the Indian telephone system she said: 'They call it crossbar but I think they mean crosswire.' At the time, that said it all.

My sisters and later, I suppose, I, were part of a handful of friends that Sanjay had. The truth is that socially he was a recluse. He detested parties and preferred to be with just one or two in a small group. However, though no real talker, Sanjay could be entertaining. He loved jokes, even though he always preferred to tell them himself. His taste in humour was often vulgar but he told his jokes extremely well. Sanjay also loved dogs and horses. At his mother's home in Delhi, he had a small kennel containing, among other dogs, two Irish wolfhounds, Sean and Sheba, of whom he was especially proud. They were the size of ponies and, though dumb and slow, pretty frightening to behold.

Sometime in the late summer of 1976, perhaps late August or early September, Sanjay asked if I wanted to go flying with him. He was a regular at the Delhi Flying Club at Safdarjung Airport, where he frequently flew a single-engine propeller plane. It had two seats, one for the pilot and one, in this instance, for a guest.

Once we had taken off and the plane had settled into a comfortable flight, Sanjay asked if I wanted to learn how to fly. Hesitantly, I accepted. What I recall is that he allowed me to occasionally put the plane into a wobble before he would laugh and correct course. His confidence made him indulgent not just of my inexperience but also my poor learning skills. However, I doubt if he was a qualified instructor. He was simply busking it.

Once the novelty of teaching a novice to fly had worn off, Sanjay began to display his own skill at aerobatics. He seemed to attempt every type of loop the little aircraft was capable of. I don't recall anything particularly dangerous but it was, nonetheless, thrilling.

By this time, we were a good distance from Delhi. Judging by the landscape, we were flying over the agricultural lands that surround the capital. Suddenly, Sanjay decided to scare the local farmers working in the fields by aiming the aircraft straight at them. As we dived towards them, their first response was to happily wave back. However, when the plane continued aiming for them, I could see the immediate change in their behaviour. They scattered in every direction as they started running, clearly scared for their lives. At the last moment, Sanjay swerved dramatically upwards. As the plane changed course and lifted skywards he looked down and waved at the perplexed lot below. He was clearly pleased with the outcome of his prank.

Whatever view one takes of such sport, it requires nerves of steel and tremendous self-confidence. Sanjay had both in abundance. It's a strange quirk of fate that he should have died in a flying accident caused by mechanical failure. Of course, we'll never know for sure whether that, in turn, was brought on by the unsafe aerobatics he was attempting at the time.

∾

I've known Aung San Suu Kyi since I was five. At the time, her mother was the Burmese ambassador in India and Suu, as I've always called her, was an undergraduate at Lady Shri Ram College. Our parents became friends and on most days Suu and my sister Kiran would drive together to college.

Madame Aung San, Suu's mother, was a warm and caring lady who loved to feed people. Khow swe was one of her specialities. My favourite was her black rice pudding.

In the early 1960s, the Burmese ambassador lived at 24, Akbar Road. Today, it's the Congress party's office. On weekends Madame Aung San would drive beyond the Qutab to feed Buddhist monks in the monasteries that existed in that area. I would often accompany her, confident in my greedy belief that I would be fed khow swe thereafter!

Even as a teenager, Suu's idealism and unrelenting commitment to her principles was the most defining quality of her character. It was one of the first things that struck you when you got to know her. She was clearly drawn to politics and knew that her future would ultimately lie in ruling Burma (the name she prefers for Myanmar). A pencil-drawn portrait that she made of my sister Kiran, dated 11 October 1962, has inscribed at the bottom: 'Kiran Thapar may be allowed entry into Burma at any time'. Suu was seventeen at the time.

I personally got to know Suu a decade later. It happened in the late '70s, when I moved to Oxford. By now married, she and Michael had a home in Park Town, not far from St Antony's. I would often drop by for coffee and a piece of cake, or Suu would ring and ask if I could babysit her younger son Kim, while she and Michael went to the movies.

A little incident from this time illustrates the sort of person she was and how she would react to any hint of racial prejudice. As usual, I was babysitting Kim, and Suu and Michael had just returned home. She suggested a nightcap before I left. We started telling jokes and I cracked one about the Chinese. Unthinkingly, I referred to them as 'Chinks'.

'You can't use that word,' she sharply rebuked me. 'It's not acceptable even in humour.' Her tone left me in no doubt of her seriousness.

Yet, this unflinching commitment to the values she considers important is, paradoxically, contrasted by her delicate and petite appearance. Suu is not just small and thin, she seems fragile. The flowers that she always wears in her hair give her an exotic touch. Her lilting speech is beguiling. So it is always a bit of a shock to hear her strong opinions. It's not what you expect from someone who seems so delicate.

In 1982, when Nisha and I were preparing for our marriage, Suu found out about the impending date from a common friend. I'd been away in Nigeria and then caught up with my new job at LWT and, as a result, we hadn't met for a couple of years.

'I hope you're going to invite me,' she rang up to ask. 'I'm the closest thing you have to a sister in London and I have to be there.' When I assured her that I would, she laughed, sensing that I was simply covering up. 'Come off it, Karan, you were never a good liar. If I hadn't rung you, you would never have phoned me.'

Suu travelled down to London for the wedding and brought Kim with her. Later, at the reception Nisha and I hosted for ourselves at the London School of Economics—Nisha's alma mater—Suu met her for the first time. When she was leaving, she grabbed my hand and pulled me aside.

'Do you realize how lucky you are?' she said. 'Nisha's not just a lovely girl, but I think she's going to keep you in check and, even if you don't know it, that's what you need!' In the years that followed, whenever she called, Suu would claim that it wasn't me she wanted to speak to but Nisha, and the reason was to find out if I was behaving myself!

When I started appearing on *Eastern Eye* on LWT, Suu would often call and talk about the stories I'd done and joke about my self-consciousness on screen. I got the impression that she made an effort to watch the programme and, whenever she did, she wouldn't hesitate to communicate what she thought about it.

Sometime in the mid-1980s—perhaps 1986 or 1987—I returned from a vacation in India to find a series of messages from Suu on the answering machine. Each asked me to ring and each sounded more anxious than the previous one. The final message simply said, 'Where are you? What's happened to you? Why won't you ring back?'

I rang her at once, wondering what had happened. It took a couple of calls before I traced her to London, where she was at the time.

'Thank God you've rung.' But when I tried to explain that I had been away on holiday and had only just returned from Delhi, she interrupted me.

'Well, you have to come over at once. There's someone you have to meet and you'll never believe who it is. I'm not going to tell you, so you have to come as quickly as you can.'

Though jetlagged, I hurried across to find out that Suu's mother was in town and, in fact, on her way back to Rangoon. Suu had been ringing for a couple of weeks because she'd wanted me to meet her. Now they were in London for a bit before Madame Aung San's return. I think I met Suu's mother on what must have been her last day in England.

'Look, Ma, look. Do you remember the fat little roly-poly? Hasn't he changed? And these days he appears on television and tells the rest of us what to think!' Suu was giggling as she said it. Her mother enveloped me in a warm embrace as she used to when I was five or six.

I didn't know it at the time, but this was my last meeting with Suu for more than twenty years. A year or so later Suu's mother fell ill. Suu dashed home to nurse her and ended up involved in politics, leading her country's popular student movement against military rule and in support of democracy. Years of house arrest and endless political struggle followed, during which time Suu was cut off from the world. For the following two decades my only contact was the unexplained phone call and the lucky interview I'd managed sometime in 1989.

We next spoke in 2011, the year she was released. We met a year later when she visited India and then again in 2015, when I flew to Rangoon to interview her.

I now saw Suu in a changed light. I realized that she had learnt to become two different people almost at the same time. During her interviews she was a politician, conscious that I was going to ask awkward questions which she was determined not to fully answer. She seemed to enjoy the cut and thrust of our exchange. This was the formal and somewhat reserved politician. But when it was over she would always say, 'Now tell me about yourself and the family. Let's have a cup of tea and catch up.' She would recall the smallest of details, the names of my entire family—including aunts and uncles I assumed she had long forgotten—as well as my hobbies and interests and the pranks I often used to get up to. Despite all that had happened, her memory and her desire to reconnect was undimmed. This was the old Suu.

That is why it's so surprising that today Suu is unable to express concern and sympathy for the Rohingyas. I realize that she has to walk a careful line between offending her country's majority Burmese population and showing concern for the Rohingya minority they despise. When I last interviewed her, in September 2015, just before the elections that brought her to power, I questioned her silence. Her explanation was that this was the only way of ensuring she would be seen as impartial by both sides. Silence gave her the opportunity and credibility to act impartially when she came to power. Her aim was reconciliation and condemnation would get in the way. It would fan the flames, not douse them.

She was speaking to me three years after the Rohingya issue first flared up in 2012 but long before October 2016 and August 2017. So I had no reason to doubt her.

Yet, this was a test she knew she would have to face sooner rather than later. The Rohingya problem is an old one that goes back to the 1940s, when they sided with the British against the Japanese, who had the support of the majority Burmese people. Indeed, immediately after Myanmar's independence, the Rohingyas tried to form a breakaway Muslim nation. Therefore, the bitterness between the Rohingyas and the rest of the country was waiting to explode. Suu has always known this.

It is also a fact that she's not president and internal security lies in the hands of the army who thwarted her claim to the top job. Criticizing them could endanger the limited power she exercises. She has to tread carefully and speak cautiously. Hers is not a positon of absolute authority. She has to compromise to survive.

Yet, not for a moment did I think that the compromise she would strike would be so tilted in favour of retaining power and influence whilst forsaking her own principles.

Today, if she speaks, it's about Rohingya terrorism and the killing of security personnel. She has nothing to say about the innocent men, women and children who have been killed in their hundreds and rendered homeless in their hundreds of thousands. Does political expediency dominate her principles so completely that she cannot even express compassion? Is she so fearful of the army that she's forgotten her own values? I didn't expect her to defy the army or endanger Burma's fledgling democracy, but I also did not expect her lips to remain so firmly sealed.

This raises a disturbing question: was her silence on the Rohingya issue before the elections impartiality, as she claimed, or seeking favour with the Burmese majority whose support she would need? Was it pragmatism or opportunism?

In the interview in September 2015 she described herself as 'a pragmatic leader'. At the time, that adjective conveyed a sense of careful balance. Today it suggests a cover for unbecoming compromise. When I asked if she was ready for the challenge of ruling Burma, she answered: 'It's a daunting challenge … I hope it brings out the best in me.' I wish I could say that it has.

8

RAJIV GANDHI AND MY RETURN
TO INDIA

It was Rajiv Gandhi who made my return to India possible. It happened in two stages and he was, I suppose, the architect of both.

First, in 1989, months after Nisha's death, when I happened to be in Delhi, Rajiv asked if I had decided how and where I would now lead my life. I said I was toying with the idea of returning home.

'But have you any experience of working in India?' The truth was, I had none. Nor, till then, had this troubled me.

'Perhaps you ought to try it out for a bit before you commit yourself to a final decision?'

'But how?' I asked.

It seemed as if Rajiv had already thought this through. He suggested that I come back and work with the Ministry of Information and Broadcasting (I&B), and Doordarshan. 'Do a trial period of three to six months and then, if this experience proves helpful and encouraging, come back for good.' This made a lot of sense and I immediately agreed.

Rajiv arranged for me to spend time in the ministry with the rank of secretary. At the time, the I&B secretary was Bob Murari. Suman Dubey was the special adviser.

These were the last months of Rajiv's tenure. With every passing week, it became clear that he was unlikely to be re-elected. This changing and febrile political environment made it easier for Doordarshan to be adventurous and, occasionally, even objective in its coverage.

I worked with a new band of reporters Doordarshan had recently recruited—young men and women keen to show their skills and prove their intellectual independence. I'm not sure if we made any impact, although some of the young people went on to make a name on the independent television channels which sprouted and then flourished a couple of years later.

My stint with the ministry and Doordarshan ended with Rajiv's defeat. To my astonishment, however, he did not forget about me.

'Well, what's your conclusion after three months?' Rajiv rang one night to ask. 'Has this experience put you off India or are you still keen to return?'

I said I was keener than ever, but I now had to look around for a proper job. After all, I needed something to do before I committed myself to coming back. But Rajiv already had the answer. He'd been in touch with Shobhana Bhartia, then the editorial director of the *Hindustan Times* and K.K. Birla's favourite daughter, and had persuaded her to set up a video magazine. This was one way of starting independent news and current affairs in India. The concept was similar to Aroon Purie's *Newstrack*, which had started making waves in urban middle-class India. Shobhana liked the idea and Rajiv suggested she should ask me to set up the venture and run it.

'Would this interest you?' Rajiv asked.

I knew this could be the only way of continuing a television career in India. My three months with the ministry and Doordarshan were sufficient to convince me that it was impossible for an independent journalist to fit into the government system without damaging his or her integrity and credibility. In the absence of independent TV channels, a video magazine that circulated through video libraries or direct subscription was the only hope of a television career. So my answer was that this made a lot of sense and I would be happy to join such a venture.

It took a few months to tie everything up, but by the early autumn of 1990 I was back in Delhi. Shobhana Bhartia's new venture was called *Eyewitness* and I was its editor-in-chief.

Those were early and exciting days for budding Indian television journalists. The members of the team I recruited were in their twenties and often fresh from college. Journalism was new to them. But they were quick learners and their diligence and natural curiosity helped shape them into sharp-eyed correspondents. At least two of the four correspondents I recruited graduated to the top of the journalist profession: Seema Chishti and Nikhil Alva. Nishtha Jain, one of our film editors, later became a top producer while Narendra Godavali became a leading cameraman with NDTV.

Eyewitness launched with a bang in March 1991, a day or so after Rajiv pulled the plug on Chandra Shekhar's minority government. This one act threw Indian politics into turmoil, thus creating a rich and fertile feeding ground for a new journalistic venture. We couldn't have asked for a better start.

However, I knew that *Eyewitness* needed stardust and spangle to attract attention. I was confident that our correspondents could deliver the journalistic goods, but we needed a recognized celebrity face to front the venture. I, therefore, wanted a co-anchor who was beautiful and well known and whose personality would act like a magnet.

Sharmila Tagore was my choice. Shobhana was a little hesitant. She wondered whether Sharmila would fit in. Would her presence soften the image of tough journalism that we wished to project? Shobhana's doubts were understandable, but she was also willing to try something new and different.

I clearly remember the day Sharmila dropped by so that I could explain what I had in mind. We chose to meet at my flat in Vasant Marg, Vasant Vihar, on a weekday afternoon for a cup of tea. I'd only just moved in and my two househelps, Umed Singh and Chander Singh, were still learning how to run a bachelor home with a certain degree of style and precision.

I was keen to make an impression on Sharmila. I knew she would be tempted to accept the role I had in mind for her if she felt comfortable with me. So I taught Umed and Chander how to lay a tray and serve tea. The truth is, I was imitating what Mummy would have done. And I was particularly pleased with the organdie napkins that I had found in a kitchen drawer. They dated back to my marriage but had never been used. With these, along with some freshly bought pastries and proper pastry forks, I hoped Sharmila would be duly impressed.

If anything, Chander and Umed were more excited than I was. After decades away from India, Sharmila's fame as a former Bollywood legend didn't mean that much to me. I knew who she was; after all, that's why I wanted her as a co-anchor. But her enormous glamour and star status were qualities I didn't fully understand. Chander and Umed definitely did.

They positioned themselves by the kitchen door, waiting for the bell to ring, both determined to dash to the entrance to let her in. I could see they were in competition.

It didn't take Sharmila long to realize the impact she was making on the two of them. I guess she'd experienced this many times before. Like a good actress, not only was she conscious of it but she willingly, if teasingly, played along.

She began by admiring the napkins and praised the servants for choosing them. I didn't dare mention that I was the one responsible. She then complimented them on the tea—which she barely touched—and almost went into raptures over the pastries which, incidentally, she didn't eat. But the act she put on—it would be unkind to call it a little bit of nakhra—cast a spell on Umed and Chander.

We were in the TV room, my favourite in the flat, and Chander and Umed now positioned themselves by the door, but just out of sight. They didn't want to miss a moment of the time Sharmila spent at our home. This, for them, was possibly the biggest encounter and certainly the closest with a major film star. They were still bachelors in their twenties. So, understandably, they were in seventh heaven.

Tea over, Sharmila decided that she wanted to see the rest of the flat. It was an unusual request, particularly since this was her first visit and she had come for a business conversation. I suspect this was her way of giving Umed and Chander a little more time to admire her.

'*Main aap ka ghar dekhna chahti hoon* (I want to see your house),' she said as she walked out of the TV room. The two of them were stunned but delighted. '*Mujhe aap dikhaoge*? (Will you show me around?)'

The two of them grinned from ear to ear. Delight was written all over their faces. But they were also so very shy. So all they managed in response was a sheepish grin.

They took Sharmila to every room in the flat. Now, fully aware that she was the cynosure of their eyes, each time she caught them looking at her she would playfully flick back her hair in a gesture that was at once both sophisticated and coquettish. I could see that Umed and Chander were thrilled.

After this I knew Sharmila would agree to be my co-anchor and, in fact, she did. However, what I hadn't expected was that most of the members of my new team—both male and female—would react to her in the same way as Umed and Chander. She bowled everyone over. In turn, they loved being around her, chatting, laughing or just being there to help.

Once Sharmila was on board, the concept of *Eyewitness* automatically altered to accommodate her and play to her strengths. Alongside the tough journalism, we decided to blend in elements of a conventional chat show. Each episode featured two celebrity guests whom the anchors, Sharmila and I, would talk to. In between our conversations, the journalistic stories would play out.

In the early days, Sharmila found the interviews she had to do daunting. She wasn't used to them, but because many were with colleagues from Bollywood she was particularly keen to make a good impression. Sparkling in front of fellow film stars was more important to her than me.

'I get nervous just before we start,' she confided. 'It's those last few moments before we begin when my mind seems to go completely blank and I panic.'

So I devised a way of distracting her as the camera director counted down to the start of the interview. Sharmila always had an earpiece on, which kept her in constant communication with me. This meant that while being offstage I could chat with her and direct the interview she was conducting. To overcome her nervousness, I decided to use this facility to make her laugh. It seemed the best way of relaxing her in that last critical minute before the interview began.

My trick was to sing the opening line of a Bellamy Brothers hit number and it never failed to make her giggle: *'If I said you had a beautiful body would you hold it against me!'*

My singing voice was no better than a croak. Yet, Sharmila would blush like a little schoolgirl and whisper back, 'Silly boy!'

But it always relaxed her and she never let me down in any of the interviews that followed.

Each episode of *Eyewitness* had something for everyone in the family: journalism, a witty chat, a performance and a quiz. The idea was to encapsulate in one or two hours what a normal independent channel would show over a whole day or even a full week. In those days Doordarshan did not accept programmes from independent producers and there were no privately owned satellite-linked television news channels. *Eyewitness* ran for nearly six years, first on video with a monthly subscription and then, after Doordarshan started to open up, as a weekly half-hour sponsored programme. Once it established itself on Doordarshan, we launched a sister programme called *The Chat Show*, which was also a half-hour weekly.

The Chat Show was a conscious attempt to introduce a programme to Indian audiences that would resemble the sort Terry Wogan, Michael Parkinson and Michael Aspel were doing in London. Each episode brought together three celebrity guests, who were either in the news because of a book or a movie or a song they had just been involved with or simply because they were fascinating people the audience would want to know more about.

In each case, the conversation was more a light-hearted chat than an interview. We would talk about their lives and, most importantly, revel in their anecdotes. The secret was to get them to tell stories. This worked because not only are stories self-contained and fun to listen to, but good raconteurs enact them and, thus, breathe another level of life into the storytelling. Finally, audiences can more easily relate to such anecdotes than they can to hard-nosed political discussions.

In 1995 *The Chat Show* won the Onida Pinnacle award. Alas, this was the only year when these awards were given. Thereafter they were discontinued and, therefore, no one has ever heard of them!

In the 1990s India was a very different country to the one we know today. The Ayodhya Mandir–Masjid dispute was at boiling point. Militancy and terrorism in Kashmir were at their height. The economic reforms that went on to transform India had just been announced and the country was in the process of being overhauled by them. On top of all this, we had a minority government and the Congress party, after decades of Nehru–Gandhi domination, had as its president someone from outside the family. He was also the prime minister.

Not surprisingly, politics and controversy dominated *Eyewitness*'s coverage. Our young correspondents enthusiastically reported on the uncertainties and insecurity prevalent in Kashmir, on the tensions and divisions centred around Ayodhya, as well as the opportunities created by the Manmohan Singh reforms. Thus, Kashmiri militants, who had till then only been spoken of, were seen and heard on *Eyewitness*; wild Hindu sadhus and obstinately, if not darkly, conservative Muslim mullahs would angrily clash on our Ayodhya footage; politicians of all stripes would be toughly questioned and often left floundering for answers. This was new to India and, even if our audience was limited, it loved our content.

On most occasions, hours after a new video was released, *Eyewitness* stories would make headlines in the newspapers. We would release an advance video to the Press Trust of India, who always gave us a good spread. In addition, we would assiduously fax our press releases to all the newspapers and often ring and encourage them to use it. They usually did. Thus, *Eyewitness* acquired a reputation and a standing that otherwise would have been difficult to conceive of.

It's hard to believe that all of this happened at a time when India was used to treating politicians with kid gloves and often placed them on a pedestal. Rarely were they available for questioning and, when they were, it was done deferentially. Questions were asked hesitantly. If they were dodged, which they usually were, the interviewees weren't pursued. Inadequate or even obviously false answers were not checked, leave aside called out. The politician was the boss and the journalist was subordinate.

It was this that *Eyewitness*—and also *Newstrack*—challenged, shook up and changed. We wouldn't just ask tough questions of politicians but often quarrel with them. We would raise issues that we knew were likely to embarrass them and then highlight their red faces and awkward silences. Even their indecorous behaviour or gauche manner was underlined and repeatedly shown.

For urban middle-class English-speaking India, this was revolutionary. Even though our journalism was not as good and our production values often weak and occasionally appalling, the audience thought that they were getting a taste of what the West was accustomed to. It made them feel good.

What we didn't know at the time was that there was a wider audience that also watched with glee. These were not natural English speakers but they aspired to be. And because the language represented a dream they wished to achieve, *Eyewitness* and *Newstrack* became a means of doing that.

Over the six years of its existence, *Eyewitness* interviewed prime ministers like P.V. Narasimha Rao, V.P. Singh and Chandra Shekhar; opposition leaders such as Atal Bihari Vajpayee and L.K. Advani, Mulayam Singh Yadav and Farooq Abdullah; a range of saffron-clad sadhus and bearded mullahs; most of Bollywood's actors and actresses; a variety of sportsmen, particularly cricketers; and a few foreign heads of government such as Benazir Bhutto and Moeenuddin Ahmad Qureshi, both of whom were prime ministers of Pakistan in the early 1990s. Although Rajiv Gandhi died within three months of *Eyewitness*'s launch, we managed three long and very revealing interviews with him.

However, the interview that I most vividly recall was with Amitabh Bachchan. Recorded in 1992, it was meant to mark his fiftieth birthday. Long before *Kaun Banega Crorepati* and even before the financial crisis that crippled his company Amitabh Bachchan Corporation Limited (ABCL), he was then both a hugely popular actor and an unblemished personality.

Although Amitabh had appeared in an earlier episode of *Eyewitness*, just months after its inauguration, this time round Amar Singh, then a director of the *Hindustan Times* and a close friend of his, had arranged the interview. Since this was a prized opportunity that would not repeat itself, we decided to do a fifty-minute interview and show it in two parts in consecutive episodes of *Eyewitness*.

The interview was recorded in the drawing room of Pratiksha, Amitabh's first home in Bombay. He was seated on a sofa with his wife Jaya beside him. His children, Shweta and Abhishek, whom we intended to talk to as well, were watching from a sofa at the other end of the room.

Everything went swimmingly until the first tape change. When we paused to enable the crew to do this, Amitabh spoke about an interview of actor Warren Beatty that he had watched on American television. According to him, what made this show riveting was the interviewer pointedly and determinedly asking Beatty about the women in his life. As Amitabh put it, everyone knew the stories, but it was magic to hear Beatty confronted with them and see his response.

I thought this was a very strange thing to tell someone who was in the middle of interviewing him. Was it a hint or a suggestion that I should do something similar? After all, like everyone else, I too had heard stories of Amitabh's alleged affairs with a number of actresses although, to be honest, I was not familiar with the details and had certainly not researched these rumours to question him about them. Still, was he giving me a message or, at least, a nudge?

The tape change couldn't have lasted more than five minutes, but it was enough to make up my mind. The temptation was too great. I decided I would take a leaf out of Amitabh's anecdote and question him the way the interviewer had questioned Beatty.

'We've just taken a pause to change tapes and during this break you told me a story about Warren Beatty,' I began. After repeating the essential details, so the audience could follow, I added: 'So let me do to you what that interviewer did to Warren Beatty. There have been a lot of stories of your alleged love affairs with actresses. After your marriage, have you had an affair with any other woman?'

If he was stunned, leave aside upset, Amitabh did not show it. My eyes were on him as I spoke and he was looking back at me equally intently. But his face was unperturbed. I don't even recall his expression changing.

'No. Never.'

'They say you've had an affair with Parveen Babi. Is there any truth to that story?'

'No,' he replied again. 'I too have read such stories. They're not true. But I can't stop magazines writing this sort of stuff.'

'What about Rekha?'

It might have been my imagination, but I thought I detected a slight movement in his eyes. He seemed to take just a little longer to reply. But when he did, his voice was as firm as ever. There was no change in his tone.

'No, not even with her.' He didn't say more. He left it at that.

Suddenly, turning to Jaya, who was still sitting beside her husband on the sofa, I asked if she believed Amitabh.

Jaya was taken aback. I could also see that Amitabh had turned his head to look straight at her as we both awaited her reply.

'I always believe my husband,' she said.

'Do you really mean that, or are you only saying it because he's sitting beside you?'

Jaya smiled. She now turned her head to look at Amitabh before she answered. 'Of course I mean it. Why should I not?'

Having exhausted what little I knew on this subject, I reverted to my planned questions and we continued the interview. It went on for perhaps another half an hour, by when I was convinced that the Bachchans had not taken umbrage at the diversion into his love life. I was even more certain of this when Amitabh insisted that the crew and I stay for lunch. Indeed, when we demurred, in the belief he was being polite, his refusal to take no for an answer suggested he was keen that we should stay. So clearly, I said to myself, he's not upset. He obviously wanted me to ask those questions and he was ready and willing to answer them.

How wrong I was. Like a volcano, anger had been building up inside him and it exploded shortly after we sat down to eat in the adjoining dining room.

It started when Jaya asked Amitabh if he would like some rice. 'You know I never eat rice,' he snapped. 'Why are you offering me something I never have?'

It sounded like an explosion. This time his face also revealed his fury. Together they charged the atmosphere. The television crew and Amitabh's children, who were with us, were not just stunned but petrified.

'I'm only offering you rice because, as yet, the rotis haven't come,' Jaya explained. She spoke very gently and softly.

'I don't want rice!' Now he was shouting. 'I never have rice and you know that. I'm not complaining that the rotis haven't come, but stop offering me rice instead.'

It was clear that this was his delayed and deflected response to my questions. That made it yet more embarrassing for us to be sitting at his table, eating his food. We were—or, at least, I was—the cause of the problem. Yet there I was, enjoying his hospitality as this spectacle played out.

'I'll just check what's happened to the rotis,' Jaya said. I'm sure she was trying to calm him but then, unthinkingly, she added, 'Why don't you have a little rice in the meantime?'

'Stop it. Just stop it,' he replied. 'I've said I don't want rice and I'm happy to wait for the rotis. Can't you understand that? What's the matter with you? Why can't you just listen to what I'm saying?'

Jaya left the room and never returned. Shortly afterwards the rotis appeared and Amitabh started eating. The rest of us, however, had no appetite left. We hurriedly ate what was on our plates and excused ourselves on the grounds that we had to get back.

For the ten or fifteen minutes we were there, I don't think anything was said. We ate in stunned silence. None of us could believe what had happened. He had lost his cool, shouted at his wife and, to be honest, disgraced himself. There was no denying or hiding this fact.

The whole thing left me confused. Part of me was embarrassed. I had trespassed into someone's privacy, lit a fuse and created confusion. However, another part of me was chuffed. My impromptu questions had clearly hit their target and even if bullseye was not delivered on screen, it was apparent for all to see at lunch.

We had barely got back to our hotel before the phone started to ring. First, it was Amar Singh. Amitabh had been in touch and told him all that had transpired. Amar Singh, who had arranged the interview, felt let down.

The next to ring was Shobhana Bhartia. No doubt Amar Singh had informed her. She felt a sense of responsibility because she owned *Eyewitness*.

When we got back to Delhi the next day, I was asked to drop the questions about Amitabh's alleged love affairs. Even though I argued that he had enticed me to put them, I was told I had either misunderstood or it was improper to probe in this way. Since I wasn't entirely sure of the propriety of what I had done, I agreed.

This meant that *Eyewitness* released the interview without the best bit! Amitabh had not said anything dramatic, but I felt that the mere fact that he was questioned about his alleged affairs would make his answers riveting, even if they were denials. However, this part was never shown.

Now, I'm not proud of what I did next, but I do believe it can be explained, understood and, possibly, forgiven. I contacted Anand Sahay, then chief of bureau of *The Pioneer*, a paper edited by Vinod Mehta at the time. Although an old paper, Vinod had revamped it and *The Pioneer* was enjoying a period of considerable success in Delhi.

My intention was to reveal the details of what had been cut out in the hope that Anand would write about it. This was my way of revealing to the world the episode I could not show on *Eyewitness*.

When it appeared, Anand's story was spread across eight columns at the bottom of *The Pioneer*'s front page. He had all the facts which, of course, he attributed to unnamed sources. Being a good writer, he had spiced it up with adjectives and structured the details in a clever way. As a result, it was gripping, widely read and much talked about.

Shobhana at once guessed that I was responsible. Although I denied it, which I had to, my tone and manner gave me away. I won't say she wasn't upset, but I'll add that it wasn't for long. And it never became an issue between us.

9

FOUR MEMORABLE PRIME
MINISTERS

I came back to India in 1990 and, over the next quarter-century, worked with a number of different organizations. First was the Hindustan Times Group, who set up a television wing called HTV and made *Eyewitness*. I was with them for seven years. The last two were as director of programmes at Home TV, a channel the *Hindustan Times* launched with partners like Pearson (who used to own the *Financial Times*), Carlton Television and Lee Ka Shek's Hong Kong-based television channel. When Home TV shut down, I moved to Sri Adhikari Brothers Television Networks Ltd for a year and then UTV for three more. Finally, in 2001, I established my own production house and called it Infotainment Television Private Limited. I've been running that for the last seventeen years.

Over all these years I got a chance to view Indian politics and, more importantly, Indian politicians intimately. I can't say that many became friends, but the vast majority are much more than acquaintances. I saw them in moments of jubilation, but also desperation and despair. I saw them struggling, but also celebrating. And I have experienced their generosity as well as their pettiness, anger and even vengeance.

These days it is commonplace to be critical of politicians. Most people claim to despise them, few respect them and only a handful admire them. Journalists and, perhaps, TV anchors in particular, bear a lot of the responsibility for the way politicians are viewed. We've exposed their underbelly—and in the process some of us have won laurels for doing so.

Yet, politicians have some rare qualities that the rest of us don't always possess. For one, they're often ready to help when you're in need. I know they gain votes or publicity from this, but the number of times they have cheerfully overlooked delays or accepted last-minute invitations and willingly replaced a guest who had ditched me at the eleventh hour are far too many to enumerate. Collectively, they do prove that they can be generous and accommodating in a way the rest of us often are not.

Politicians are also usually great raconteurs. In addition, they have an ear for gossip. Together, this means they can be engaging company. An evening with a politician bubbles with the recounting of scandals and rumour, anecdotes and exaggeration, and a multitude of jokes.

As a result, they are very convivial. Even those who don't drink are rarely shy. They like the limelight and have acquired the art of knowing how to stay in it.

Perhaps the best way of recounting the twenty-eight years I've worked in India as a television anchor is by writing about some of the politicians I got to know and my stories about them.

∾

It might seem like an odd thing to say in the second half of the second decade of the twenty-first century, but politicians in the 1990s, who were often inaccessible and usually unwilling to or, at least, inexperienced at giving interviews, were rather friendly once you got past the front door. Consequently, I got to know prime ministers like V.P. Singh, Chandra Shekhar and Atal Bihari Vajpayee rather well, the first two after their brief stints in office and the third years before he got there.

However, the first sitting prime minister I interviewed was P.V. Narasimha Rao. It happened just twenty-four hours after he was sworn-in and the lady who made it possible was his confidante, Kalyani Shankar. The fact that I knew Rao wasn't enough for me to get an interview once he had become prime minister. Kalyani, however, knew him far better.

At 6 in the morning the day after Rao's swearing-in, Shobhana Bhartia rang up to ask if I wanted to interview the new PM. There was no question of my saying anything other than a very eager and enthusiastic yes.

'Well, ring Kalyani,' she said. 'She can wangle it for you. She'll probably arrange it for later today.'

'Are you sure? As fast as that? This is his first day as prime minister!'

Shobhana laughed. At the time I had no idea how close Kalyani was to Narasimha Rao and, therefore, how powerful that made her. 'Kalyani can manage anything. Give her a ring and find out for yourself.'

To my astonishment, Kalyani told me to arrive at the PM's house which, at the time, was 9, Motilal Nehru Marg, at 1 p.m. When I said that the security guards wouldn't let me in, Kalyani brushed aside my concerns and told me not to worry about little things like that.

So, the crew and I arrived sharp at 1. The prime minister wasn't home. I presumed he was still in office. The guards, however, were expecting us and we were waved through. When the car pulled up at the porch, Kalyani was there to receive us.

'Would you like to do some filming before the PM comes?' she asked.

When we agreed, she took us straight to his bedroom. It wasn't just simple; it was spartan. The four legs of the niwaar bed had bamboo rods tied to them and they sported a mosquito net on top. This was uncannily similar to the 'machchhardanis' I remembered from Doon School. Along the wall on the other side of the room was a bookshelf and, adjacent to it, a rather large computer. Leaning against the bookshelf was a tennis racket and a tin of Slazenger balls.

Never before—and, indeed, never after—have I been taken to a prime minister's bedroom and allowed to film whatever I want. The crew realized this was an opportunity that even the PM might not have granted had he been there. So they started filming immediately and pretty comprehensively.

As they did so, I noticed that hanging from the top of the mosquito net were three or four of the prime minister's underpants. I assumed they'd been washed the night before and left to dry. The cameraman was the first to notice and quick to film them.

I perused the bookshelf. I noticed several books in Spanish. There were also a few on tennis stars of the past. The one I remember was on the 1960s Wimbledon champion Manuel Santana.

Half an hour or so later, by when we had finished filming the bedroom and other rooms, such as the drawing and dining rooms, the prime minister arrived. For a man whom I had thought of as soft-spoken, reticent and even shy, he seemed in a rather good mood. Best of all, he was unaccustomedly chatty.

'I can't answer political questions because I've just taken over but I'm happy to talk about other things. Would that be okay?'

So we sat down in his drawing room and he proceeded to reveal details of his life and personality that no one had known of or even guessed at. I can't say Narasimha Rao came across as a lively or bubbly human being, but it was fascinating to discover that he spoke six or seven languages fluently, including Spanish, and was passionate about tennis. But what was really surprising was that he had a dry and subtle sense of humour.

'I noticed a computer in your bedroom,' I asked. 'I had no idea you were one of Rajiv Gandhi's computer young boys.'

'In my case, that would have probably been one of Rajiv's computer old men!' he replied.

The political interview that Narasimha Rao had said would happen later on did not materialize for two-and-a-half years. But when it did, the timing was perfect and more than made up for the delay. Once again, Kalyani was the 'midwife'.

It happened in early December 1992, a few days after the collapse of the Babri Masjid. At the time many people felt that nothing had shaken India as this one event had. More significantly, it had damaged the prime minister's authority, if not also his credibility. The popular view was that he had been caught sleeping on the job and, whilst he slumbered, the mosque had been attacked and demolished. This was, therefore, the greatest challenge Narasimha Rao faced and an interview at this time would be a coup for any journalist. Not surprisingly, there were thousands trying for one.

Narasimha Rao agreed to two television interviews, one for Doordarshan done by Dileep Padgaonkar, then editor of *The Times of India*, and one for *Eyewitness* by me. The interview was confirmed the evening before, which gave us roughly twelve hours to prepare. It was recorded in the gardens of 7, Race Course Road.

It was a bright, crisp but chilly winter day and the wind kept blowing Narasimha Rao's shawl off his shoulders. So, in addition to battling my questions, he also struggled to keep his shawl wrapped around him. This made him look the way he no doubt felt—an unhappy man.

Narasimha Rao had a lot to say and, because he was a carefully measured speaker, he took his time saying it. But nothing actually critical was said in response to my questions about how or why he had let the mosque collapse and, more importantly, the personal responsibility that fell on him. He either avoided these questions or simply refused to answer to the point. Nonetheless, he was the prime minister and he was speaking about the most important event of the last thirty years; so virtually everything he said made news. Consequently, this interview established *Eyewitness* as a credible and authoritative political video magazine. But few people knew that it had been possible only because Kalyani was his friend and had convinced him to agree.

∾

V.P. Singh and Chandra Shekhar were people I got to know after their fall from power. I had heard that V.P. Singh was a poet, artist and videographer. That was my convenient excuse when I asked him to agree to a documentary profile. He readily accepted.

We must have devoted three or four days to this project, enough time to get to know the person. Once I had won his confidence, he gave me access to his collection of paintings and his poetry. He seemed particularly pleased when the cameraman started recording him filming flowers in his own garden.

Till then I had known him only as a politician and, like many others, thought of him as an astute if not crafty tactician. The person behind the politician was unknown.

Singh's poetry was in Hindi, therefore I'm not equipped to assess it. But his paintings were striking, both in terms of their colour and the images they portrayed, while his video documentaries revealed a light-hearted humorous side that was so different to the serious and often silent politician. The one that I vividly recall is of a dog on the veranda of his house looking out at the heavy monsoon rain. What brought it to life was the soundtrack he had added. It was the song '*How much is that doggie in the window?*' I think he was rather proud of this.

By the time the crew finished filming, Singh and I had become friends. On my last day he suddenly said to me: 'Now it's my turn and you can't say no.' Another of his hobbies, he revealed, was photography and he wanted to take pictures of me.

We agreed to do it on the following Sunday but then, inexplicably, I forgot. A phone call at 11 in the morning from his office reminded me that I was expected half an hour earlier. The problem was that I was unshaven, wearing an old pair of jeans and, worst of all, my hair had been oiled. My plan had been to play squash in the afternoon and then take a thoroughly well-deserved bath. All of that was now thrown out of the window as I rushed to V.P. Singh's house.

He must have taken a hundred pictures. He seemed unconcerned by my appearance or the fact that my hair was greasy. His biggest problem was to get me to smile or laugh and do so naturally. Whenever I tried he would wince, claiming that it looked artificial.

When he finished two or three hours later, Singh declared that he had perhaps a handful of decent pictures and promised to send me the best. It arrived after a week. It's a mugshot with the cheesiest grin on my face, huge teeth flashing out from between my lips. And there's nothing to hide the greasy mop of hair on my head.

'This is exactly what you look like,' Singh said when I rang to thank him for the picture. He was rather pleased with it. I, however, was convinced that this was his revenge. When I put that to him, he merely laughed.

'Ask anyone and they'll tell you this is how you really look.'

Singh was an enigma for most people during his life. Many did not know what to make of him. Some saw him as a canny politician, others as a man of high principle and a few as a misfit.

But behind the political facade he was a warm human being with a finely developed aesthetic sense and a gentle manner. Sadly, he chose to keep that hidden from all but a few close friends and the odd lucky journalist.

∾

I got to know Chandra Shekhar in rather strange, if not also unpropitious, circumstances. He was prime minister when *Eyewitness* was launched and the opening episode had an interview with him. This got us into a terrible fight but once resolved, it also made for a firm and lasting friendship.

The interview was just a ten-minute affair conducted by one of the more promising correspondents on the *Eyewitness* team, Savyasaachi Jain. I knew it had to attract attention, otherwise the first episode would not make a mark. I, therefore, decided that it had to go beyond the normal conventional political questions. I asked Saachi, as Jain was called, to question Chandra Shekhar about his clothes and general appearance.

At the time, it was unheard of to question the head of government along these lines. In Britain, where I had come from, this would be taken as good fun. In India, it was seen as impertinence. Actually, downright rudeness.

Saachi loved the idea and together we devised a set of questions designed to catch the audience's attention. He first asked Chandra Shekhar why he was so careless about his appearance. Indians, his question began, make it a point to appear well-groomed; mothers send forth their little sons with their hair carefully combed, faces scrubbed and eyes highlighted with kohl. Chandra Shekhar, on the other hand, appeared as prime minister in a dhoti that was often crushed and hair that was windswept and uncombed. Surely, this wasn't the right image for the PM?

Chandra Shekhar growled in response. I don't think he could believe what he was hearing. He had never been questioned in this way. When Saachi persisted, he turned and looked away. However, that didn't disguise his anger, nor did it make him more willing to answer.

Undeterred, Saachi pointed out that Chandra Shekhar's sartorial appearance and general manner were more akin to the hippy tradition than what traditional Indians considered a fitting way for a prime minister to present himself. This, of course, added fuel to Chandra Shekhar's anger, which was clearly visible on screen. Mercifully, he didn't walk out, but he was seething by the time the ten-minute interview got over.

Chandra Shekhar complained to Shobhana but the interview, when it released, was widely talked about. That, after all, was my intention. So, from the limited perspective of *Eyewitness*, it was a significant success.

Days later, Chandra Shekhar lost power and became a caretaker prime minister. Three months after that, post the elections, he was replaced by Narasimha Rao. It was at this point that Amar Singh stepped in and changed our relationship.

'Do you intend to be a foe of Chandra Shekhar forever?' he suddenly asked me. 'Or, now that he's out of office, are you willing to make up?'

It had never been my intention to pick a fight and I certainly did not want to be Chandra Shekhar's enemy forever. Amar Singh's suggestion not only made sense, it also opened the opportunity to get to know Chandra Shekhar better. If nothing else, I was curious about the man.

So I accepted Amar Singh's offer to make peace and, shortly afterwards, accompanied him to Chandra Shekhar's for tea. It was probably his last day at 7, Race Course Road. I could see he was relieved that he was departing. The last few months had been particularly difficult. First, there was the economic crisis, which led to the mortgaging of India's gold reserves. Then there was Rajiv Gandhi's assassination and the postponement of the second stage of the election process. Now that it was all over, he was only too happy to hand over the burden of running the country to someone else.

Amar Singh's presence made the meeting a lot easier. He's an ebullient and chatty person and carefully managed the conversation for the first few minutes while Chandra Shekhar and I became comfortable in each other's presence. It didn't take us long to get to that point. Soon we were swapping anecdotes and laughing.

An hour later, when I was departing, I asked the former PM if he would be willing to do a long, reflective interview on Indian politics from the standpoint of someone who has seen it over the decades, first as a Young Turk in Indira Gandhi's Congress party, then as president of Janata Party and, finally, as prime minister. It wasn't my plan to ask for this. It just came into my head as I was leaving. Chandra Shekhar clearly liked the idea and readily agreed.

The interview was done a week or so later and recorded at his farm in Bhondsi, outside Delhi. He spoke with remarkable candour. His criticism of Indian politics and politicians rang with the truth of personal experience. Even if some sensed bitterness in his tone and manner, it was undeniable that he spoke as no previous prime minister had ever done before. Chandra Shekhar held up a mirror to Indian politics and the reflection confirmed what many had suspected: it can be dirty, brutal and, often, devoid of principle.

Over the next few years I did several more interviews with Chandra Shekhar. In the process, we established a bond that worked for both of us. There were times when I knew no one else would speak on a particular issue, and would ring and ask him to step into the breach. He would do so willingly. On other occasions, when he had something to say but was unsure if others would telecast it without editing, he'd call and I would happily provide the platform he wanted. Of course, on both sorts of occasion, Chandra Shekhar always made news.

I remained in touch with Chandra Shekhar till his death, though the frequency of our meetings did diminish. But each time we met, his welcome would be warm and his laugh unrestrained. Though a principled socialist, he was also a bon viveur. He loved a good chat and this made him engaging company for a young, aspiring journalist.

∾

I got to know Atal Bihari Vajpayee because of the kindness of the lady he spent his life with and whose daughter he considers his foster child—Mrs Kaul. I'm not sure why but she took a shine to me and whenever I wanted an interview she would ensure that Atal-ji said yes.

The funny thing is, it always seemed to happen the same way. I would ring Raisina Road, where Atal-ji lived in the early '90s, and leave repeated messages asking to speak to him. I have no idea what would happen but he would rarely, if ever, ring back. Then, after my fifth or sixth attempt, Mrs Kaul would come on the line.

The first time this happened I was rather embarrassed. I thought she had taken the phone to admonish me for my persistence. It certainly was beginning to feel like pestering. So I began by stammering my apologies.

'Oho, oho,' she interrupted and shut me up. 'You have every right to call, beta, and I know what you want. Let me speak to him. Give me a day or so. *Ho jaana chahiye.*'

I have to confess that I was sceptical. I thought she was fobbing me off. How wrong I was! When I called back the next morning it was to hear her say, with a chuckle in her voice, that the interview had been fixed. She told me to come that evening and added that Atal-ji had agreed.

I have no doubt that I owe Mrs Kaul a huge debt of gratitude. Without her repeated interventions, the many interviews I did with Atal-ji would never have happened. They included the only one he did after the Babri Masjid demolition as well as another exclusive, six months later, when four BJP state governments in Rajasthan, Madhya Pradesh, Uttar Pradesh and Himachal Pradesh that had been dismissed by the prime minister after the masjid demolition, failed to get re-elected.

The BJP slogan at the time was '*Aaj panch pradesh, kal sara desh*' (Five states today, the entire country tomorrow). I began my interview by mischievously repeating this to him. Of the five states, the BJP had lost four and so the prospect of winning the nation had receded very badly.

Atal-ji laughed. His face broke into a huge smile and his eyes twinkled. I wasn't sure if it was mischief or glee. He had a very winning appearance when he was smiling. One's heart automatically warmed to him.

'*Aaj panch pradesh, kal sara desh*,' he repeated and laughed again. He didn't need to say more. It was clear he was poking fun at his party's braggadocio.

While conducting these interviews, my task was to draw him out. If I ever felt the need to challenge him, I would do so gently because I didn't want to make him defensive and put him off. By and large I succeeded in my goal because most people thought the interviews were eye-opening and, more significantly, they made headlines the next day.

I think I'm right in saying that in the early '90s Atal-ji felt comfortable with me and I had his trust. The first confirmation of this was just after Rajiv Gandhi's death in 1991. *Eyewitness* had planned a special obituary for Rajiv. Our idea was to invite a multitude of people who knew him and ask them to share their most important memory. The aim was to capture something of Rajiv's personality and the impact he had had on people. When I approached Atal-ji, his initial response was to ask me to meet him before he made up his mind.

What followed was an extraordinary conversation that led to a unique and touching moment in our obituary.

'I'm happy to speak about Rajiv,' Atal-ji began. 'But I don't want to speak as a leader of the opposition because that would not permit me to say what I really want to. I want to speak as a human being who got to know a side of Rajiv that perhaps no one else in public life has seen. If that is okay with you, I'm happy to be part of the obituary you are planning.'

I wasn't sure what he had in mind. It sounded intriguing but I needed to know more. So I asked him to tell me what he wanted to say.

Apparently, during the early part of his prime ministership, Rajiv Gandhi had learnt that Atal-ji had a kidney problem and needed treatment. So he summoned him to the Prime Minister's Office in Parliament and said that he intended to make Atal-ji a member of the Indian delegation to the United Nations. He hoped that Atal-ji would accept, go to New York and get treated. And that's what Atal-ji did. As he told me, this possibly saved his life and now, after Rajiv's sudden and tragic death, he wanted to make the story public as a way of saying thank you.

Now, this is not the way politicians from opposite sides of the fence usually speak of each other. If ever they do, it's only in private. Atal-ji's determination to do so publicly was not just unusual, it was truly unique. More importantly, this was heartfelt gratitude. The story touched a chord within me and I knew it would have the same effect on the audience. It was likely to be the most important bit—the high point, if that's not an inappropriate term—of the obituary.

I readily accepted. We recorded the next day and Atal-ji spoke exactly as he said he would. However, the impact he made was far greater than the actual content of what he had to say. His slow, measured delivery and the obvious emotion that lay behind it made an unforgettable impression on everyone.

When I thanked him for this magical moment, he instead thanked me for giving him the opportunity to say something that he had long wanted to express but didn't know how to. He said that a weight had been lifted off his mind.

The second occasion when I sensed a special relationship with Atal-ji was during his prime ministership. I had been invited to a banquet at Rashtrapati Bhavan for the president of Guyana. I was standing at one end of Ashoka Hall along with all the other guests when Prime Minister Vajpayee who, because of his weak knees, always used the lift, entered the room from the other side. As he walked across the floor, a hush descended on the gathering. Everyone was looking at him as he slowly but steadily crossed the enormous room.

Suddenly, halfway across, he gestured with his hand as if he was summoning someone out of the forty or fifty people at the other side. Since no one knew whom he was signalling, several people took a couple of steps forward. This made Atal-ji laugh and everyone who had moved forward stepped back and returned to where they were.

However, Atal-ji continued to summon. It was then that I suddenly felt he was calling me. So I moved forward again and he confirmed that I was right by pointing straight at me.

With everyone watching, I walked across the carpet to talk to the PM. Just a day or so earlier I had written a column critical of him and I wondered if he had read it.

'*Aap ka lekh maine padha tha* (I read what you had written),' Atal-ji began. But he was laughing. Perhaps he was teasing. Still it made me feel awkward, if not guilty.

'Atal-ji,' I blurted out. 'My mother read it too and told me I'm an idiot.'

'*Ma hamesha galat nahi hoti* (Mothers aren't always wrong),' he said and roared with laughter.

Then he put his hand on my shoulder and chatted for another minute or two. I knew at once that he wasn't in the least bit upset. It took me just a little longer to realize that the PM was also sending a deft message to everyone else. Many of them would have read what I had written and were perhaps wondering how he would react. This display of friendliness was also meant to set their minds at rest. It was smart proof that the PM didn't mind criticism. Like a good democrat—and a wise politician—he was visibly rising above it.

For me, this was abiding proof that Atal-ji is not just a good man but also an astute politician. With the smallest of gestures, he could send the biggest of messages. And he had the ability of doing so in the most natural of ways. This was just one example. In his political career of several decades there must have been thousands more.

10

L.K. ADVANI: THE FRIENDSHIP AND THE FALLING-OUT

I have no doubt that the BJP politician I've got to know best—and through him his family as well—is Lal Krishna Advani. There was a time when I had clearly won his confidence and, on the odd occasion, he would even accept my advice. In the process, he allowed me a glimpse of the secret inner working of Indian politics and Indo-Pakistan diplomacy.

Our relationship began—and matured into friendship—because of the many interviews I did with him. Initially I had no other reason to meet him but because he readily agreed to my interview requests, they became more frequent and in the process I got to know him better and better. It's therefore ironical that it was an interview that also snapped the bond of friendship and virtually ended our contact with each other.

My first interview with Advani was in 1990, when he was leader of the opposition and I an unknown journalist recently returned to India. It was intended for the inaugural episode of *Eyewitness*. In those

Daddy   Mummy   My cowboy years.

Loreto Convent, Tara Hall, Simla.

Report.   Miss/Master....Karen Thapar....................................

Term.......................................   Form.... Lower Infants ....

No in Form ....   Place in Form...

Subject		Remarks on work of Term
Reading ...	...	Too young to concentrate. Can do well if he tries.
Spoken English ...	...	Speaks clearly
Geography ...	...	-
Hindi ...	...	-
Nature Study ...	...	-
Writing ...	...	Not very keen on writing and too young to insist on this.
Number work ...	...	Good but will do better when he settles down more
Spelling ...	...	-
Hand work ...	...	-
Drawing ...	...	-
Drill ...	...	Satisfactory
Recitation ...	...	-
Singing ...	...	Fair

General Report on

Work and conduct.

Mother M. Helena.
Superior.

Struggling to learn.

As a roly-poly six-year-old at my elder
sister Premila's wedding.

Abo

Mummy and my three sisters, Premila, Shobha and Kiran.

When two queens met: my mother with Queen Elizabeth II.

The Jaipur House debating team. I am standing second from the right. Next to me (second from the left) is Vikram Seth.

Chandos House, Stowe School, 1974. I am seated in the second row, sixth from the left.

Pembroke College, Cambridge

Union picks new president

The 21-year-old son of a former Commander-in-Chief of the Indian Army, Mr. Karan Thapar, is to be next term's president of the Cambridge Union.

A lifelong friend of the Ghandi family, Mr. Thapar has so far been unable to persuade Mrs. Indira Ghandi to visit Cambridge.

But with a promise from the UN Secretary-General, Dr. Kurt Waldheim, and definite bookings from many British politicians—including Lord Home, Mr. Jeremy Thorpe and Mr. Reginald

Maudling—Mr. Thapar's debating and lecture programme for next term is now nearing completion.

A former champion debater at the Cambridge Union and a popular chairman of debates, Mr. Thapar said today he was confident the society would surmount its present financial problems.

Some remoulding of its image might be necessary, he said, but in the long run a stronger and more lasting Cambridge Union would emerge.

Karen Thapar

My presidency announced in the *Cambridge Evening News*, 1976.

Looking smug at the Cambridge Union.

Proposing my presidential debate motion at the Cambridge Union, March 1977.

Presiding over the Cambridge Union.

Cambridge Union, Lent Term, 1977. Adrienne Corri speaking.

Sprawled across Benazir Bhutto's car in Cambridge.

Benazir Bhutto speaking at the Cambridge Union to propose the motion 'That art is elitist—or it is nothing'. I chaired the debate as president of the Union.

Union head denies romance

The Cambridge Union President, Mr Karan Thapar, an Indian, today denied reports linking him romantically with the Pakistan President's daughter, Miss Benazir Bhutto, and said the rumours could jeopardize her father's national election chances next week.

The official denial, he said, was issued because he feared for the consequences such reports could have for President Bhutto in suggesting a link between his family and an Indian.

Miss Bhutto is an undergraduate at Oxford where she is President of the Union. Mr Thapar is a member of an eminent Indian political and military family and son of a former chief of the Indian Army.

He issued the statement at the Cambridge Union today after repeated contacts from British and overseas pressmen, following an evening out in London with Miss Bhutto.

"It is a quite ridiculous suggestion and there is absolutely no truth in it. My main concern is that a week before his election President Bhutto could be placed in an embarrassing position if it is widely reported that he has family connections with Indians, who are, after all, in many respects traditional enemies of Pakistan."

Mr Thapar left Cambridge at midday yesterday to meet Miss Bhutto in London.

Mr Thapar said today: "We had a very enjoyable evening and it is quite true that Miss Bhutto is coming shortly to stay in Cambridge. But romance—no."

Refuting rumours, *Cambridge Evening News,* 1977.

THE CAMBRIDGE UNION SOCIETY

FOURTH DEBATE

LENT TERM, 1977

MONDAY, 31st JANUARY, 1977 8.15 p.m.

"That Politics is an Honourable Profession"

MR. MICHAEL HART, Emmanuel College, will propose.
MR. COLIN HARNETT, Emmanuel College, will oppose.
MR. CHRISTOPHER GOODALL, Magdalene College, will speak third.
MR. PETER LUFF, Corpus Christi College, will speak fourth.
RT. HON. MICHAEL STEWART, M.P., will speak fifth.
PROF. BERNARD CRICK will speak sixth.
RT. HON. JEREMY THORPE, M.P., will speak seventh.
MR. MICHAEL LEAPMAN will speak eighth.

Tellers:

FOR THE AYES	FLOOR :	FOR THE NOES
ANN ELLIS (New Hall)		LOUISE SOMERSET (Girton College)
CHRISTOPHER IRELAND (C.C.A.T.)	GALLERY :	PAUL APLIN (C.C.A.T.)

Pembroke College   KARAN THAPAR, *President*

THE CAMBRIDGE UNION SOCIETY

TENTH DEBATE

LENT TERM, 1977

FRIDAY, 25th FEBRUARY, 1977 8.15 p.m.

"That Art is Elitist—or it is Nothing"

MR. ADRIAN SELLS, Christ's College, will propose.
MR. NICHOLAS HYTNER, Trinity Hall, will oppose.
MR. GUY THOMPSON, Sidney Sussex College, will speak third.
MR. JON BAKER, St. John's College, will speak fourth.
MR. JEREMY BLACK, Queens' College, will speak fifth, from the cross-benches.
MISS BENAZIR BHUTTO, President, Oxford Union, will speak sixth.
MISS ARIANNA STASSINOPOULOS, ex-President, will speak seventh.
MR. TOM KEATING will speak eighth.
MR. CLIVE JAMES will speak ninth.
MR. YEHUDI MENUHIN, K.B.E., will speak tenth, from the cross-benches.

Tellers:

FOR THE AYES	FLOOR : CROSS-BENCHES :	FOR THE NOES
MR. WILLIAM D'ARCY (Trinity College)	MISS ROSEMARY MOORE (Newnham College)	MR. CHARLES STEPHEN (Queens' College)
MR. JEREMY THOMAS (Christ's College)	GALLERY :	MR. CHRIS ANSELL (C.C.A.T.)

Pembroke College   KARAN THAPAR, *President*

THE DEBATE WILL BE FILMED BY THE B.B.C.

METRO — UNION — SOCIETY

proudly presents

"THE ELEVENTH DEBATE OF TERM" x

LENT TERM, 1977

THURSDAY, 3rd MARCH, 1977, 8.15 p.m.

"A Drink before and a Cigarette after are Three of the Best Things in Life"

MR. ANDREW DALLAS (ex-Bar Manager), Emmanuel College, Vice-President, will propose.
MR. ADAIR TURNER, Gonville & Caius College, C.U. Yak Society, Secretary, will oppose.
MR. MARK TURVEY, Maudlin College, Standing Committee, will speak third.
MR. JOHN "PINKO" PEARSON, Girton College, will fall over.
MR. NIGEL HAMSTER will speak fifth.
MR. PHILIP NORMAN, of the *Sunday Comics* and other strips, will speak sixth.
MR. HUGHIE GREEN will speak most sincerely, folks!
MR. MICHAEL PARKINSON, "An old-fashioned Humbug," will speak eighth.

Tellers:

FOR THE AYES	FOR THE NOES
The return of	
REV. MOSES WILDEBEESTE, PH.D. (Strath Clyde)	MR. KARL AARDVARK ...ofessor of Inhumanities (C.C.A.T.)

Monday, 28th February, 1977
Pembroke College of Art & Technology

KARAN B. THAPAR, Jnr.
Producer

CAMBRIDGE UNION SOCIETY

and

OXFAM   present

Ravi Shankar (sitar)

IN CONCERT Accompanied by

Alla Rakba (tabla)

King's College Chapel

By kind permission of the Provost and Fellows

Monday 17th. January 8·00pm

TICKETS: £2·50; 2·00 (£1·50 members); 75p (60p members)
FROM: Union Society Office, Bridge Street (61521)
Oxfam Office, 110 Regent St., Central Library Box Office, Lion Yard

---

(Top left and right, and bottom left) Some of the Cambridge Union debates during my presidency, Lent Term, 1977.

When Ravi Shankar performed at King's College Chapel, Cambridge.

Joss sticks burn at King's

1,000 pack chapel to hear Indian virtuoso

Joss sticks burned in King's College Chapel, Cambridge, last night when a capacity audience of more than 1,000 heard a recital by the world-renowned Indian sitarist, Ravi Shankar. The performance was a sell-out, even after the promoters, the Cambridge Union Society, had increased by 190 the number of seats available. A total of 1,190 were eventually put on sale.

The recital was in the ante-chapel with Mr. Shankar and his accompanists seated on a specially erected dias covered with traditional Indian rugs and surrounded by electronic recording and amplifying equipment.

But the failure of members of the audience to arrive on time delayed the start of the recital by nearly an hour. Ravi Shankar, who had earlier indicated to organisers that he wanted no disturbance during his playing.

The effect of the sell-out was to boost the Union Society's £500 target profit to an unexpected £750, all of which has been given to Oxfam, co-sponsors of the event with the union.

The money is to be devoted to a West Bengal children's orphanage—West Bengal is Ravi Shankar's home state.

Before mounting the dias for last night's recital, Shankar commented: "My favourite places for playing are always temples and churches. King's is a very fine place for such music and we are delighted with the acoustics."

He added: "This is the third time I have been to Cambridge and I am very happy to be here. It is a beautiful place."

The Cambridge Union president, Mr. Karan Thapar, himself from Delhi, who first mooted the idea of large-scale charity performance organised by the society, said: "I am absolutely delighted with the way everything has gone.

Joss sticks burn as Ravi Shankar tunes his accompanist's tamboura. 1377723

A report in the *Cambridge Evening News* about the jam-packed recital by Ravi Shankar, 1977.

Liberal Party leader Jeremy Thorpe performing an Utthita Padmasana pose in my digs.

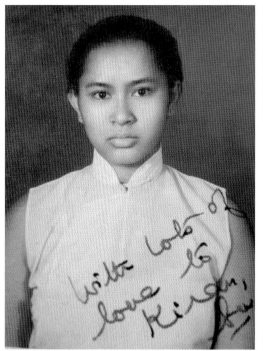

Aung San Suu Kyi at eighteen.

A visa for Burma for my sister Kiran
from Aung San Suu Kyi herself.

With Aung San Suu Kyi after an interview in November 2012.

With my presidential debate guests, Cambridge Union, March 1977.

Graduation from Cambridge, 1977.

St Antony's College, Oxford, October 1977. I am seated third from the left in the front row. At the time, I used to keep a beard.

Nisha at our wedding, 3 December 1982.

The picture former prime minister
V.P. Singh took of me in 1992.

Nisha, shortly after she agreed to marry me.

Benazir in front of the television lights, some time around 2003.

V.P. Singh filming flowers, 1992.

P.V. Narasimha Rao struggling with his shawl, December 1992.

A relaxed Rajiv Gandhi in 1990 during his interview.

A smiling A.B. Vajpayee after an interview.

L.K. Advani during one of his many *HARDtalk India* interviews.

J. Jayalalithaa's heated interview in 2004.

When Narendra Modi decided to walk out during the 2007 interview.

The Bachchan family before the *Eyewitness* interview in 1992.

Sachin Tendulkar enjoying the interview, 1999.

Kapil Dev in tears during the interview in 2000.

Interviewing General Pervez Musharraf in 2006.

With Barack Obama in 2017.

With Amal Clooney, during the India Today Conclave, 2016.

days, Doordarshan did not accept programmes from independent producers and there were no privately owned satellite-linked television news channels. But at the time *Eyewitness* was an unknown entity and I wasn't sure if Advani would accept. Fortunately, he did.

The interview took place on a pleasant December afternoon at his Pandara Park residence. It wasn't very long, probably ten or twelve minutes. It appeared in March 1991 when the first episode of *Eyewitness* was launched.

A short time later, when I next met him, I asked him what he'd thought of the interview. He tersely replied that he had been told it was a travesty. Then he abruptly turned and walked away.

Stunned by this behaviour, I sent him a VHS of the interview and asked him to see it for himself. I was confident that he had been misled.

Weeks, actually months, went by without any response. In fact, I gave up expecting one. Then suddenly, late one summer evening, the phone rang. It was L.K. Advani.

'Karan, I've just seen the interview and there was absolutely nothing wrong with it. I was clearly misinformed. However, I'm too old to make that excuse and I'm afraid I behaved badly when we last met. I'm ringing to apologize.'

This unhesitating willingness to accept a mistake is perhaps his greatest quality and immediately attracted me to him. Over the years that followed, I've seen it on many occasions. The one that stands out was February 1998, when, as president of the BJP, he was campaigning for the elections. During one of his halts in Delhi he agreed to an interview with me.

On that occasion, my intention was to question the sincerity of the new, genial and appealing image the BJP was projecting. Was this the true character of the party or just a facade to dupe the electorate?

Halfway into the interview and just before we paused for the commercial break, I said to Advani: '*Aapne rakshas ke seengh ukhaad ke munh pe muskarahat dal di hai. Lekin ye dikhava hai ya asliyat?* (You have changed your image from demonic to genial. Is this an act or for real?)' I'm not sure why I asked this question in Hindi—the interview was, of course, in English. It just came out that way.

At the time Advani did not react adversely. However, a few minutes later when we took the break, he got up, saying that he didn't want to continue. The crew and I were stunned. When I asked what the problem was, he replied with a question of his own: 'Why do you want to interview a man you consider a rakshas?' I realized I had hurt him, which was not my intention.

Moments later, Advani left the room. But then, within a flash, he walked back in. He had barely been out for a minute. Resuming his seat and looking at the crew, he apologized for what he had just done. 'I'm sorry, I shouldn't have done that. You have come all the way to interview me and the least I can do is finish the interview. Let's continue.'

Fortunately, when the interview ended we were friends again. I knew that on occasion Advani can be quick to anger or get hurt easily, but he is usually even faster to forgive and forget. At such times his eyes well with tears. For me, that's a sign of how transparent and honest his emotions are.

Seen in this light, it's not surprising that Advani agreed to give me his first interview as home minister. It happened on the first day he attended office in South Block. Actually, on the morning after his swearing-in, he had to fly to Kerala for the funeral of E.M.S. Namboodiripad, a highly regarded communist leader. This meant that his second day as home minister was the first time he walked into his office and took formal charge of his ministry.

I had been in touch with Pratibha Advani throughout the preceding day to ensure that her father would give me an interview. Near midnight she confirmed he would, adding that he wanted the crew and me to come to South Block by 9 in the morning.

Advani didn't say anything exceptional. As a new home minister, he was guarded and aware that what he said would be heard attentively and reported widely. But the fact that he gave an interview on his first morning in office was recognized by many. This otherwise unexceptional half-hour was, therefore, also well watched.

It was, however, a strange turn of events that took our relationship from politician and journalist to something approaching friendship, which also included his family. It had nothing to do with journalism and everything to do with the fact that the Pakistani high commissioner in India, Ashraf Jehangir Qazi, was a dear friend of mine and determined to make a serious effort to alter the fraught relationship between our two countries.

Eager to establish a personal rapport with the National Democratic Alliance (NDA) government, Ashraf asked if I could help. George Fernandes was my initial choice and I set up a few meetings for them, usually over quiet dinners at my home. That worked magnificently. Fernandes and Ashraf became friends and learnt to trust each other. But Fernandes, Ashraf quickly realized, could not influence the government on the tricky issue of Pakistan. That could only be done by a BJP leader who, additionally, was trusted by Prime Minister Vajpayee.

'I'd like to meet Mr Advani,' Ashraf announced one day in early 2000. George Fernandes, who recognized and accepted the need, arranged the meeting and I was asked to drive Ashraf to Advani's Pandara Park residence. It was fixed for 10 p.m. No one else was informed.

Ashraf had no idea how long the meeting would last. 'Don't go far,' he warned me. 'I'll ring your mobile as soon as it's over.' I sat outside in the car, expecting him in half an hour. He stayed for ninety minutes.

Over the next eighteen months, there were perhaps twenty or thirty such clandestine meetings. The vast majority took place at night. I would be the chauffeur and the guards at Pandara Park were only given my name. The whole thing felt like a cloak-and-dagger game in a B-grade Bollywood film.

The only person who stumbled upon this—but I don't think he worked out what exactly was happening—was Sudheendra Kulkarni. In those days, he was Vajpayee's speech writer. His association with Advani was yet to begin. At the first meeting between Ashraf and Advani, he walked in unannounced to deliver papers and caught all of us having a chat after the formal meeting was over. Fortunately, Sudheendra didn't linger. Nor did he suspect anything.

Two weeks later, when the second meeting was underway and I'd parked under a street light in Khan Market, Sudheendra, emerging from a Chinese restaurant, saw me and walked up to ask what I was doing.

'I'm a little early to collect a friend who's dining at the Ambassador Hotel,' I lied. 'So I thought I'd wait here.' Amazingly, Sudheendra believed this but it was a close thing.

I had been lucky on two consecutive occasions, but everyone involved knew I couldn't risk a third. Pratibha and Mrs Advani insisted that, hereafter, I wait with them while Advani and Ashraf talked in the former's study.

Soon a routine was established. The two As would disappear into Advani's study. I would sit with Mrs Advani and Pratibha. When the meeting was over the other two would join us for a cup of tea.

Late in May 2001, India announced that it had invited General Pervez Musharraf for a summit in Agra. At 6.30 the next morning Advani rang. I was asleep. 'I'm sorry for calling so early but I want you to tell our common friend that he shares the credit for this development. Our meetings were a big help.'

Their last meeting took place during the Musharraf visit. It happened after the Rashtrapati Bhavan banquet, close to 11 p.m. Ashraf rapidly changed from his achkan into casual clothes so that no one would recognize him. Advani still had on the grey trousers of his bandgala suit. The Agra summit was due the next morning. There was hope in the air.

In the end, the summit failed. Ashraf's and Advani's best efforts were in vain but the bond they formed did not snap. It lasted through the difficult months of the attack on Parliament in December 2001 and the Kaluchak terror attack in 2002, which led to Ashraf being asked to leave. Though no longer a go-between, I continued to witness the amazing relationship between Advani and Ashraf that few, if any, knew about. I recall two further occasions that were both remarkable and showcase their friendship in a fascinating light.

The first was on Friday, 14 December 2001, the day after the attack on Parliament. Chandan Mitra, the editor of *The Pioneer*, was celebrating the tenth anniversary of the newspaper. His party on the lawns of The Imperial was going to be the first big social occasion after the shocking Parliament attack. In turn, that would probably be the only subject of discussion as politicians and journalists mingled with each other. Not surprisingly, I was looking forward to it.

Around noon that day Ashraf rang up for a chat. He wanted to know what people were saying about the attack on Parliament. I suggested that he accompany me to Chandan's reception. There couldn't be a better way of finding out.

'Do you think I should?' he asked. Ashraf is a naturally gregarious person. Such reticence was out of character. But that day, I could understand his hesitation. In his shoes I would have felt the same.

'Of course you should,' I replied. 'No one holds you personally responsible or feels anything against you.'

Ashraf hesitated, but then agreed. Perhaps he accepted my point or perhaps he saw the evening as a challenge he had to face. Maybe it was both.

At 8.30 I picked him up and together we drove to The Imperial. Chandan's party was outside on the lawns and the weather was decidedly nippy. There were groups of people standing around scattered angheetis. We headed for one that seemed central but not crowded. As I scanned the other guests, I noticed the Advani family entering from the other side. Mr Advani was in front, escorted by Chandan. Mrs Advani, Pratibha and his son Jayant were just behind.

One by one, journalists started to head for Advani. The previous day, he had been holed up inside Parliament as terrorists invaded the complex and fired on the building. Twenty-four hours later, he seemed relaxed. He was smiling, laughing and chatting. I decided to walk up and find out what those horrible hours the day before had been like.

'I'm off to meet Mr Advani,' I said to Ashraf.

'I'll wait here,' he replied. We both instinctively knew that that was the sensible thing to do. This was not an evening for forced politeness, leave aside awkward encounters.

As I worked my way through the crowd in Advani's direction, I suddenly felt a hand on my shoulder. I turned to find Mrs Advani. My eyes had been fixed so firmly on her husband that I hadn't noticed her until we almost bumped into each other. But before I could apologize or even start a greeting she spoke to me.

'*Aapne apne dost ko peeche kyon chhod diya* (Why have you left your friend behind)?' she said, smiling broadly.

'*Mera dost* (My friend)?' I questioned, momentarily fazed.

'*Qazi Sahab. Abhi to aap unke saath khade the* (You were just standing with him).'

Mrs Advani had seen us. Despite her smile, my heart sank. I wasn't sure if this was a rebuke. Did she feel I had erred in keeping the Pakistan high commissioner's company on that night?

'He feels a little hesitant to come forward,' I said.

I was surprised by how easily I blurted that out. It's not as if Ashraf had said as much, but I knew that's how he felt. You get to know a person after being close friends for years. But I was still surprised

I had said this in front of Mrs Advani. Normally I try to be more circumspect.

If anything, Mrs Advani's smile grew broader still. As I spoke, her eyes seemed to light up and before I could finish, she appeared to have made up her mind.

'*Ismein kya personal cheez hai?*' she said. '*Aur phir aapke dost hain. Woh nahin aate to main jaake unse milti hoon* (There's nothing personal. And he's your friend. If he won't come forward, I'll go meet him).'

And before I could respond she started walking towards Ashraf. I followed hastily. It didn't take more than fifteen seconds but in that time my head was awhirl with conflicting thoughts. Mrs Advani, the Indian home minister's wife, the man who only the day before had been trapped inside Parliament by terrorists we were convinced were trained and funded by Pakistan, if not actually Pakistanis themselves, was going to meet the Pakistani high commissioner. Others in her place might have preferred to snub him or, at least, keep away. I couldn't think of another soul—minister, minister's wife or ordinary guest—who would have sought him out that evening. Nor would Ashraf have expected them to. And I know that he would have understood if he had been ignored. Yet here was Mrs Advani striding towards him, smiling as she did, unconcerned about what the world would say or think.

The look on Ashraf's face when he recognized Mrs Advani and realized that she was coming to meet him was indescribable. In fact, for a moment I don't think he knew how to react. At first he looked completely taken by surprise. Seconds later, he looked totally delighted. He could not have imagined this in his wildest dreams. Such things don't happen in conventional politics or diplomacy. In fact, a politician or a diplomat would have carefully avoided such a meeting.

This is why Mrs Advani's gesture was so special. It wasn't a political act and it had no political message. It was a warm human gesture and much more meaningful. It was the response of a sensitive soul, reaching out beyond the strictures of politics to show friendship at a difficult but telling time. The easy thing would have been to do nothing. No one would have remarked on that. It was risky to show personal concern at a time when it could so easily be mistaken for something else. None of that worried Mrs Advani. She consciously chose to put a human relationship above politics, above prejudice and above the risk of public misperception.

In fact, she even encouraged Ashraf to meet Mr Advani, which he eventually did. Mrs Advani was confident that her husband would greet the Pakistani high commissioner graciously. She wasn't wrong. Ashraf hovered in the vicinity of the home minister, uncertain whether to go forward or not. Suddenly, Mr Advani spotted him and, with a cheerful smile on his face, stepped forward and clasped the high commissioner's proffered hand in both of his own. It was another moment that evening when human warmth transcended the cold compulsion of politics. No doubt on the morrow, politics would return to the forefront as it would have to, but on the evening of the fourteenth the Advanis showed that there was room for personal gestures and that individual relationships still mattered.

If anything, the second meeting between Ashraf and Advani was more extraordinary. In fact, it was the last time they would meet while the former was the country's high commissioner. It happened six months after the encounter at The Imperial and just days after the terrible terrorist attack at Kaluchak in Jammu in May 2002. Leaving thirty-one dead and forty-seven wounded, this was one attack too many for the Indian government. The Indian high commissioner had been withdrawn from Pakistan several months earlier, but the Pakistanis had not asked Ashraf to return and the Indians had not pressed for his departure. But now the Vajpayee government asked for Ashraf to be withdrawn and gave him a week to leave the country.

Long before the Kaluchak attack, Ashraf had sensed that his time in Delhi was coming to an end. He had wanted to make a difference and, at first, his relationship with Advani suggested that that might just happen. But after the failure of the Agra summit and the attack on Parliament he knew that wasn't going to be the case.

As the seven days given to him ticked by, I got a call from Mrs Advani asking if I would bring Ashraf and his wife, Abidah, for tea on their penultimate evening. The Advanis wanted to meet the Qazis and personally bid farewell. This was an amazing gesture by the deputy prime minister of a government that had just chosen to declare Ashraf persona non grata. Of course, this wasn't publicized. That would have embarrassed the Advanis. But they went ahead, knowing the story could leak out.

This was also one of my last duties as Ashraf's chauffeur. I drove the Qazis to the new Advani home—they had recently moved from Pandara Park to Prithviraj Road. We had tea in the study. It was just the Advanis and Pratibha and, of course, Ashraf, Abidah and me.

I can't remember the conversation but there was, no doubt, a strain in the air. After all, both parties were aware of the circumstances that were bringing their relationship to an end. After half an hour, the Qazis got up to leave but unbeknownst to them there was one touching surprise still in store. It happened when Ashraf approached Advani to shake hands.

'Galey lago,' Mrs Advani intervened. Both men were taken aback. They stared at her. 'Galey lago,' she repeated. And then, almost as if this was what they both wanted, Advani and Ashraf embraced.

I was standing behind Ashraf, so I could clearly see Advani's face. Tears had welled up in his eyes.

Advani wasn't the only member of the Vajpayee government to take an unprecedented step to bid Ashraf and Abidah farewell. An even bigger gesture, in a sense, was made by George Fernandes who, at the time, was defence minister.

Jaya Jaitly, his confidante, rang to ask if I would bring Abidah and Ashraf to dinner on their last night in Delhi. The Qazis had, in fact, planned a farewell reception for that evening but when they heard about George Fernandes's invitation they decided they would slip away from their own party by 8.30 p.m., even though most of the other guests would be lingering on.

I collected Abidah and Ashraf from The Taj, where the reception was being held, and drove them to George Fernandes's residence in Krishna Menon Marg. George greeted them at the front door with a warm hug and a big smile. A bit of that, no doubt, was to cover up the awkwardness everyone felt.

It was just George and Jaya, Abidah and Ashraf, and me. I hadn't expected it but George insisted that Ashraf have a drink. He produced a bottle of Scotch and when Ashraf demurred, poured the drink out himself.

This cheered everyone up and we reminisced over drinks, reminding each other of earlier meetings and earlier dinners. By the time we sat down to eat, everyone was completely at ease. And by the time coffee was served, we were like old friends exchanging jokes.

It was well past midnight before the Qazis got up and we started to leave. George and Jaya came up to the car. They stood and waved as we drove out of the house.

'Who would believe that you've been asked to leave the country?' I said to Ashraf as we headed towards the Pakistan High Commission. 'What a strange world we live in.'

'Yes,' he said. He sounded reflective. 'But it also shows that George and Advani can reach out beyond politics and make a difference. This dinner and yesterday's tea are two occasions I will never forget.'

∾

It's hard to say how much of the credit goes to Ashraf—though some certainly does—but Advani's attitude to Pakistan started to change after meeting him. I could detect it in his tone and manner, rather than his language. His references to the country seemed softer, even gentler. Then, a while later, I noticed that he seemed to recall his time in Karachi more often. Anecdotes from those days played an increasing part in his conversation. And each time his face would light up.

However, the first concrete proof that Advani's outlook on Pakistan had changed came when the Pakistani foreign minister of the time, Khurshid Kasuri, visited Delhi in 2005. Advani was leader of the opposition and also president of the BJP. It was in that capacity that Kasuri called on him. During their conversation the Pakistani minister extended an invitation to the Advani family to visit his country.

Coincidentally, I had scheduled an interview with Kasuri for 10 p.m. the same night he called on Advani. Around 4 or 5 that afternoon, I received a call asking if I could meet Advani in the early part of the evening. I wasn't told what he had to say and I had no idea what to expect.

When I met him, Advani told me about the meeting and the invitation to visit Pakistan. He wanted me to convey his answer. I'm not sure why he chose me and didn't respond more formally. He did not explain and I didn't ask.

Advani said that he would be delighted to visit Pakistan and would like to do so with his wife, daughter, son and daughter-in-law. I passed on the message when I met Kasuri that night. I'm not sure if he had expected such a swift reply, but he immediately called for paper and asked me to write down the names of Advani's children. I did so.

The foreign minister seemed pleased. His intention was to take one of the most hard-line BJP leaders to Pakistan in the hope that exposure to the country and its legendary hospitality would change Advani's attitude and soften his politics. He could not have known that, in fact, this had already been happening.

Things moved pretty swiftly hereafter. A formal invitation was issued to the Advani family, which they accepted, and the visit happened a few weeks later.

On the day of his departure, I sent Advani a short personal letter to wish him good luck. I ended by pointing out that I've always believed there is a little bit of India in every Pakistani and a little bit of Pakistan in every Indian. This sentiment clearly struck a chord because the Pakistani papers reported that Advani said something very similar during his visit to the Katas Raj Temple complex outside Lahore.

Unfortunately, Advani's Pakistan visit led directly to the loss of his BJP presidency. It happened because of what he wrote in the visitors' book at the Jinnah mausoleum in Karachi.

'There are many people who leave an inerasable stamp on history,' he wrote in the register. 'But there are very few who actually create history. Quaid-e-Azam Muhammad Ali Jinnah was one such rare individual.'

In his early years, Sarojini Naidu, a leading luminary of India's freedom struggle, described Mr Jinnah as an 'ambassador of Hindu-Muslim unity'. His address to the Constituent Assembly of Pakistan on August 11, 1947, is really a classic, a forceful espousal of a secular state in which, while every citizen would be free to practice his own religion, the state shall make no distinction between one citizen and another on grounds of faith. My respectful homage to this great man.

His words were unexceptional but the BJP and, more importantly, the Rashtriya Swayamsevak Sangh (RSS) could not accept his calling Jinnah secular. It went against their grain. I'm not sure if they were anyway looking for an opportunity to move him out but this certainly gave them the excuse to do so.

However, Advani's inscription reminded me of my own view of him. I've always believed that he's a liberal and secular man who uses religion for political or strategic purposes. Ironically, Jinnah was similar. Neither man was prejudiced against people of other faiths. Indeed, Jinnah wasn't particularly religious and I'm not sure if Advani is either. No doubt he's a believer, but the rituals and practices of Hinduism play little part in his behaviour and outlook.

Although losing the BJP presidency may have hurt, it didn't change Advani's attitude towards Pakistan. The gentler, softer outlook continued. He also never recanted or withdrew the words he wrote in the visitors' book. Whenever we spoke about it, he always maintained he'd written the truth.

By 2006, I felt quite close to the Advanis. Little did I realize this was soon to end and it would all happen very abruptly. Now, when I look back on it, I can admit that the fault was probably mine.

Around March that year, I asked Advani for an interview for *Devil's Advocate*, the CNN-IBN programme I used to anchor at the time. Rajnath Singh had taken over as BJP president and I had formed the impression that he had significantly altered the position the party had taken on critical issues under Advani. I thought that this would be the ideal subject and Advani would want to talk about it. Alas, I was wrong.

The interview took place in the drawing room at Prithviraj Road. Mrs Advani and Pratibha were sitting out of camera view but carefully listening. This was normal practice. In addition, their presence always relaxed him. However, I ensured that they were not in his line of sight because I didn't want him to look in their direction for confirmation or affirmation of what he said. On screen that would look odd.

We got through the interview and it was only when it was over that Advani said he wasn't happy. He didn't say why but I sensed that he didn't like the line of argument that his successor had overturned his position on many important issues. Perhaps it reopened a wound that had not fully healed.

Advani asked if I would redo it. He was happy to talk about any subject but, in retrospect, he felt it was wrong for him to have spoken about his successor. In contrast, I felt I had got a good interview and, like any possessive journalist, did not want to lose it.

In response, I suggested that Advani should consider the matter for a day or so. After all, the interview would not be broadcast for another three days. He said he would, but he also indicated it was unlikely he would change his mind. It was on this basis that I left his home.

I now found myself in a difficult position. The interview had been recorded and the tapes were in my possession. But I had also given Advani the feeling, without saying it in so many words, that if a day later he still wanted the interview redone, that was a possibility. I hadn't said I would agree, but the possibility I might was not ruled out. That was the unspoken understanding when I left the Advanis' home.

Advani didn't change his position. He rang early the next morning to say he didn't want the recorded interview to be telecast but was ready to do another one. I still found that difficult to accept. Advani then called up Rajdeep Sardesai, the editor of CNN-IBN, to ask him to intercede. An embarrassed Rajdeep suggested I should think again. Was it worth upsetting Advani and damaging a good relationship over one interview?

I should have listened to Rajdeep's advice. Indeed, I should have listened to Advani's plea. I was well aware that not just this interview but many earlier ones as well had been granted because Advani considered me a friend. He trusted me. I would add that he liked me. This made him comfortable and the interviews I got were a direct result.

So now, if he wanted an interview dropped but was willing to give another in its place, was I putting a somewhat manufactured journalistic principle ahead of a trust and friendship I had benefited from for years and which was the reason I had got the interview in the first place? If I had thought along these lines, I would have acted differently. I should have, but a certain adamantine hardness crept into my thinking and I became rigid.

Once I insisted, Rajdeep agreed to broadcast the interview. My last hope was that Advani would see it on air, hear the viewers' response and, perhaps, accept that the interview was okay and his reservations were mistaken. But that was not to be.

Thereafter, relations did not just cool, they snapped and ended. If we met at some public venue, he would smile and shake hands, Pratibha would embrace me, but it was no longer the same.

It took me a while to realize that I'd made a mistake. That in my folly I had lost a valuable relationship. But when I did come around to accept the fact and try to make up for it, I discovered it was too late. I asked to meet Advani several times and he would always politely hear me out. He'd offer tea and we would talk of other things but the curtain that had dropped refused to rise again.

Three years later, in 2009, as the campaign for the national election got underway with Advani as the BJP's prime ministerial candidate, Pratibha arranged a long interview with her father, once again for *Devil's Advocate*. The excuse was that this was intended as the first of a series with top politicians in the run-up to voting but, more importantly, it was an attempt to build bridges and wipe out the past.

I planned a two-part interview. Part two would be about the policies that an Advani government might follow in terms of domestic issues as well as foreign affairs. I knew he would be happy to talk about this. Part one, however, was about the problems he would face getting elected and, more awkwardly, the behaviour and comments of some of his BJP colleagues which had attracted adverse attention.

I should have recorded the interview in reverse order. Part two first, because that would have relaxed him and removed the apprehensions that were still lurking in his mind. After that, it would be easier to raise the awkward questions contained in part one. But I only realized this after beginning the interview in proper chronological order and by then it was too late.

Ten minutes into part one, Advani got up and left. I had not said anything to upset him and the issues I'd raised and questions I'd asked would have been unexceptional if voiced by someone else. From me, however, they brought back fears that I might repeat 2006 again. I believe this was the concern that made him get up and end the interview.

This time both Mrs Advani and Pratibha said I had done no wrong. They tried to convince Advani to return and continue. But it didn't work.

I was left with ten minutes of an unfinished interview and it was never aired. In desperation, I rang up Arun Jaitley who agreed to fill the breach. But my relationship with Advani and his family was clearly over.

Since 2009, I have seen very little of the Advanis. He did, however, agree to an interview in 2015 to mark the fortieth anniversary of the Emergency. Nothing went wrong on this occasion but it wasn't an exciting interview either.

Later in 2015, Advani and Pratibha accepted an invitation from my sisters to attend a garden reception they were hosting at the Gymkhana Club for my sixtieth birthday. The moment they told me they had invited him I knew he would come. This is the sort of courtesy and gesture he considers important and always fulfills. And when he came, he was warm and gracious. But that was the politeness of a gentleman.

Now the older I get, the more aware I become that I made a terrible mistake and paid for it by losing Advani's friendship. But you can't undo what's done. Once paths diverge, they go in different directions. Hereafter, that's the way it will be.

11

THREE STORIES ABOUT
PRANAB MUKHERJEE

I lost touch with Pranab Mukherjee after he became president of India in 2012. After all, a journalist can't go knocking on the doors of Rashtrapati Bhavan and expect to be let in, or pick up the phone and natter with its exalted occupant. But in the decades before that, I felt I had established a relationship which revealed some of his remarkable qualities.

Pranab Mukherjee can get angry quickly, but he's faster to forget and forgive. During an interview in 2004, for the BBC programme *HARDtalk India*, recorded at Jamia Millia Islamia University, when I began by repeatedly and forcefully questioning his decision as defence minister to promote to lieutenant general a man who had been rejected on three separate occasions by an army board and suggested this was politicization of the army, he was visibly riled. When I then questioned if he had done this because the officer concerned was related to a senior Congress leader, his face became incandescent. I could see his veins throbbing. Finally, when I said that this contradicted Dr Manmohan Singh's pledge to 'recapture the spirit of idealism' and his 'commitment to decency (and) morality', Mr Mukherjee's fury made me fear he might walk out.

He didn't. Instead, we changed the subject and carried on talking for another twenty minutes. When the interview ended, I apologized for annoying him. His response took me completely by surprise.

He threw back his head and laughed. His eyes were twinkling and I could see that this wasn't put on. 'You were doing your job and I was doing mine,' he said. 'I've known you long enough, Korron (as he fondly mispronounces my name), to realize that your bark is worse than your bite.'

Then, with his hand on my shoulder, we walked down Jamia's long corridors to his waiting car. He wanted everyone to know that he wasn't upset. More importantly, he didn't ask for any cuts.

Years earlier in 1995, when his unwarranted 'banishment' from high politics had ended and he was Narasimha Rao's foreign minister, I had met him for an off-the-record briefing prior to an interview for *Eyewitness* with Benazir Bhutto who was, at the time, Pakistan's prime minister.

'You know what to ask, Korron,' he said, brushing aside my reason for calling on him. 'I would like you to take a message to her.'

In turn, she gave me one for him and I thus got a second opportunity to meet him. This proved very useful because Salman Haidar, then India's foreign secretary, refused to clear the interview with Benazir for broadcast by Doordarshan. In those days that was a huge stumbling block.

'Hmmm...' Mr Mukherjee responded when I told him how the interview was stuck. 'I don't want to embarrass the FS by overruling him. Why don't you give it to a private channel and I'll ensure there is no further obstacle?'

That's exactly what I did. BiTV telecast the interview and Vir Sanghvi held a series of discussions about its content. It ended up garnering more attention than it would have on Doordarshan.

My last story involving Pranab Mukherjee is to do with the 26/11 attacks that happened in Mumbai in 2008. Mr Mukherjee was, once again, external affairs minister. At the time, on 28 November, someone had made a hoax call to Pakistan President Asif Zardari, claiming to be Pranab Mukherjee, and got through. This caller, it was said, had threatened Zardari. The Pakistanis raised the matter with Washington and Condoleezza Rice, then US secretary of state, telephoned Mr Mukherjee for clarification in the middle of the night.

On 29 November, the day 26/11 ended, Asif Zardari gave me an interview. A few hours later, when I rang to thank him, he gave me a message for Mr Mukherjee. 'Tell him not to threaten me in future. This is not the way a foreign minister should behave.' It took me a while to contact Mr Mukherjee and he heard me out in silence. When I finished, he made me repeat the story a second time. 'Thank you, Korron,' he said, but I sensed the episode wasn't over.

Hours later Satyabrata Pal, then our high commissioner to Pakistan, rang with a full explanation and details to prove that the call that had upset Zardari was a hoax. I was asked to pass this on to the Pakistan president. I can't say that Asif was convinced, but he was prepared to consider the matter closed. 'Forget it,' he said and laughed. 'There are more important things happening in the world. Give Mr Mukherjee my regards and make sure you tell him I'm a good guy.' When I did, Pranab Mukherjee simply giggled.

Mr Mukherjee is a good-hearted man who bears no ill will. He's a wise politician who can help a journalist without embarrassing a civil servant who has erred. Finally, he can handle awkward situations with deft discretion and no one will ever know how he did it. He's also always in firm control of what he's saying. I've never known him to be indiscreet, unless it is deliberately so. He gives you the feeling that not just his life, but possibly every minute of it, is carefully planned or, at least, well considered and easily accounted for.

12

WHEN I MADE KAPIL CRY AND SACHIN TALK

Unlike practically every other Indian, I'm not enthusiastic about cricket. In fact, it bores me. So, not surprisingly, I'm also ignorant of the finer points of the game. The wonderful names for placement on a cricket field mean nothing to me. I can't identify a crafty spin from a fast-ball attack or a cover drive from a cross-bat shot.

My lack of knowledge of and utter disinterest in the game used to make Mummy distraught. She was an enthusiastic cricket fan and particularly fond of the West Indies XI. When a Test match was on, she could spend all five days in front of the TV fortified by her cigarettes and frequent cups of coffee.

It wasn't so much my inability to play the game that she found difficult to accept as my indifference to it. 'There's something definitely wrong with you,' she would say and shoo me out of the room so that she could watch undistracted by my foolish comments.

Yet the paradox is that I've done multiple interviews with cricketers and they've often turned out to be rather watchable. This is despite that fact that my first one for *Face to Face*, with Rahul Dravid, just after the cricket World Cup in 1999 where he was the highest run-getter, was perhaps the worst start anyone could have. The research I had been given showed that Rahul had failed to score a century by just five runs during his debut in 1996. My producer at the BBC, Vishal Pant, suggested that I should begin by asking what that felt like. Of course I agreed.

'Let's start with your debut,' I began. 'What did it feel like to miss a century in your first Test by just five wickets?'

'Five runs!!!' Rahul roared back, laughing loudly. At the time I had no idea how foolish I seemed, but that became unavoidably apparent when the interview went on air and the world discovered that I knew nothing of the game.

However, it's the interview with Kapil Dev in 2000 that made headlines across the cricketing world. It's an interesting story—and one I'm keen to tell—but if I begin with it, I'll convey a misleading impression of Kapil. So let me go back in time to the days when I was a young journalist with LWT.

I first met Kapil Dev in 1983. It was the morning after the World Cup victory. The shock and the surprise had not yet dissipated. The joy and euphoria were only just setting in. The cricketing world was in a trance. Our winning team was on cloud nine.

'Of course, of course,' he said as I followed him down the hotel corridor, asking for an interview. He was surrounded by interview-seeking journalists. I must have been one of fifty. His answer to each was similarly encouraging and reassuring.

I wasn't convinced that he meant it. Perhaps he was being polite or maybe he was trying to get rid of us. So I started telephoning to reconfirm. I rang the hotel, his room, the lobby, the dining room, his alleged friends. You name the number, I must have called it. Eventually, well past midnight, I got through.

'Haan yaar,' he cheerfully replied. 'It's tomorrow morning at 9, but why don't you let me get some sleep before that!'

Kapil was on time and brought his vice-captain, Mohinder Amarnath, as well. They were sleepy, perhaps a little hungover, but happiness infused the interview. It was the first I handled as an associate producer at LWT. It wasn't faultless but it was memorable.

It was this easy helpfulness that struck me about Kapil. Stars can be prima donnas and often reluctant to assist lowly mortals. Not Kapil. In March 2000, when I was making programmes for the BBC, I encountered the same quality again. We were scheduled to interview Sourav Ganguly. It was the day before the Faridabad One-day game with South Africa. Sourav had agreed, the time had been fixed but he was running late. The clock was ticking and I was beginning to fear the interview might not happen. With stars, silly accidents sometimes disrupt the best-laid plans. Just then I got a call.

'Hi Karan,' a voice crackled over my mobile phone. '*Main Kapil Dev bol raha hoon* (This is Kapil Dev.)'

'Oh, hi,' I replied, stunned and somewhat speechless. Why was he ringing me?

'Suno, Sourav is with me and if you want your interview, pick him up from my office in the next ten minutes.'

When I got there, a beaming Kapil had Sourav ready, dressed and waiting. The look on my face must have suggested that I was perplexed. How had Kapil swung this? How did he even know about the proposed interview?

'I heard your conversation with Sourav on the mobile and realized you were panicky and I decided that this was the only way to do it,' he explained. 'Had Sourav returned to the hotel to change, you would never have got him.'

So Kapil took him to his office and made him shower, shave and dress there. The interview that followed was a gem but few people outside my circle of colleagues realized that Kapil had pulled it off.

And now to the interview that took the world by surprise. The paradox is that it happened almost by accident. At the time, Kapil was the highest wicket-taker in the world and, of course, had been the captain of India's World Cup-winning team. I called on Kapil on Thursday, 4 May 2000, to ask for an interview.

The BBC had asked us to do a series of *Face to Face* interviews with great cricketers of the present and legends of the past. These were to be personality pieces—soft, gentle, anecdotal. Kapil wasn't very keen. Just days before I met him, *Tehelka* had published allegations suggesting that Kapil had accepted Rs 25 lakh to throw a cricket game. The story had been picked up widely and everyone was talking about it. It was clearly on his mind. So the invitation to do a soft feature interview did not excite him. Yet, the idea of doing one for the BBC was something he warmed to.

'*Suno yaar*,' he said, as he poured me a cup of tea. 'Let's do a proper one. You ask what you want and let me answer the way I think I should.'

It took me a few seconds to realize what Kapil was proposing. He was agreeing to be interviewed, but not for a gentle personality series. He wanted to be on the tougher *HARDtalk India*, to face the most difficult questions possible on the charges he was accused of. He was, in fact, giving me a scoop.

'When?' I asked tentatively, apprehensive that fixing a date might clip the soaring hopes he had just created.

'Tomorrow? Day after? The sooner the better.'

The recording was fixed for midday the following Saturday. Kapil arrived wearing shorts, although he had brought a jacket and formal shirt to wear on top. He thought he would be visible only from the waist upwards, so this was all he would need. But the interview contained a couple of wide shots where his hairy legs are clearly visible.

From start to finish, the interview was about the allegations he faced. For the first ten minutes he took my questions squarely on the chin. He seemed unruffled and undisturbed. But when I asked if he was worried about the fact that history might remember him not just as the captain of India's World Cup-winning cricket team or the highest wicket-taker, but also as someone accused of accepting money to throw a match, a dam inside seemed to burst and his emotions poured out in a flood of tears.

It happened so suddenly, it took me aback. Tears rolled down his cheeks, his voice began to quiver and then actually broke. His nose started to run. In fact, he was crying like a baby.

Watching Kapil, I knew I had a moment of television magic on my hands. Years earlier, I had been told that the two most gripping things on TV are children laughing ecstatically and adults unable to control their tears.

I know it sounds heartless, but the first thought that came to my mind was that the interview still had fifteen minutes to run and it would be an anticlimax if Kapil's tears were to dry up and his manner return to normal. I instinctively felt I had to ensure that he continued to cry till the end. Yet I was also aware that if I played with his emotions and asked questions which would prompt further tears it would look and feel terribly wrong. I would lose the audience and ruin the interview. So I dropped my voice to sound concerned and sympathetic, but continued to ask tough questions. I continued to probe the allegations and question his answers as well as their veracity.

This worked. Kapil's tears flowed relentlessly.

Looking back, I'm not proud of what I did. But I'm not embarrassed either. I had a job to do at the time, and it was to get the best interview. If this meant prolonging Kapil's tears, so be it.

I knew the interview would attract attention but I had no idea what that would actually amount to. The BBC had hired a marketing agency and one of their staff, Sunil Kalra, was in the production box watching the recording. So he was aware of what had happened and the first thing he did was to offer an exclusive with pictures of a crying Kapil to the *Hindustan Times*. The next day, Sunday, was the paper's day of biggest circulation. Its front page was emblazoned with four pictures of Kapil in tears. The story underneath provided details of what had happened.

The interview had still not been broadcast—and would not be for a further week—but it had already made front-page headlines. It wasn't long before the BBC itself picked up excerpts to run in their news. All the other Indian papers ran stories of their own. *Outlook* magazine made it a cover story. They took a screenshot from the interview, which shows Kapil crying and rubbing his right eye with his right hand in a futile effort to stop his tears. His face is not just distraught, it suggests a man having a complete emotional breakdown.

The night the interview was broadcast, I must have received a hundred calls asking the same question: Were Kapil's tears real? Or was it dramebaazi, to use the colloquial Hindi expression?

Let me start by assuming that the emotion was put on. Theoretically it could have been, but then Kapil would have to be an actor—not a simple Bollywood product but one of Shakespearean proportions. To cry as he did on demand is not easy. Most of our actors cannot or, at least, not convincingly.

That leads me inexorably to the conclusion that the tears were genuine and the emotion real. I interpret them as the cry of an anguished soul, expressing both pain and helplessness. If I were in his position, it's possible I would behave similarly too. But were they also tears of remorse? I don't think so, but of course, they could have been.

〜

The other cricketer whose interview left a deep impression on me is Sachin Tendulkar. This was for *Face to Face*, recorded in 1999, a year before the Kapil interview and just months after the one with Rahul Dravid.

Sachin was at the peak of his fame but still a young man, shy and very unused to television. Getting him to agree to the interview was the first problem. My letters to him went unanswered. Any phone numbers I was given turned out to be wrong or the calls were not returned. It was only when I met Mark Mascarenhas, his publicity manager, and discovered that Mark had known Nisha and her parents, that my luck started to turn.

Mark spoke to Sachin, recommending the interview, and it was fixed in days.

Thereafter, Vishal Pant spoke at length to Sachin's wife Anjali and collected a host of delightful anecdotes spanning his entire life. Our intention—as was the case with all *Face to Face* interviews—was to get Sachin to talk about himself and his life and we believed that this was best done by telling stories.

Vishal explained to Anjali that this was important for three reasons. First, the audience could easily follow and identify with the stories. Second, most people tend to become animated or dramatic while narrating anecdotes and that enlivens an interview. Finally, if it's a good story, it's remembered and retold, giving the interview a further lease of life.

Anjali understood and promised to prime Sachin. We arrived in Bombay twenty-four hours before the recording. Anjali had suggested that we should drop by that evening to meet Sachin. She felt it would relax him and added that it was important to put him at ease if we wanted to get the best out of him the next day.

Vishal and I went together and found Sachin and Anjali waiting for us. The two of us must have spent over two hours with the two of them.

Sachin had several questions and I sensed at once that it was important not just to answer them but also to reassure him that he had fully understood what was required of him the next day. So I shared the questions we had and, more importantly, identified the stories we were looking for in response to each of them. Vishal added that these were things Anjali had told him.

In several cases, Sachin wanted to tell a different story to the one Anjali had given or tell that one in answer to a different question. In other cases, he had better stories and preferred to go with those. These were not just acceptable changes; I was convinced they would make for a better interview on the grounds that people are always better at telling stories they want to relate rather than those that others want to hear from them.

Before we left, Sachin asked if we could do a trial run so that he could get the hang of it. We did and it was immediately clear he knew how to tell a story. He's a raconteur, on top of an ace cricketer.

The next day, the interview was at the New Oberoi Hotel. Sachin drove himself in a red Mercedes sports car which the hotel permitted him to park smack bang at the entrance.

I had a twenty-five-minute interview in mind only to discover that overnight, Sachin had thought of many additional anecdotes for several of the questions. He now had a cornucopia of stories to share. So the interview continued for just under an hour.

I decided not to curb or restrain him because I felt we might lose out on a story we had never heard before and which could be better than the one we were expecting. And, certainly, Sachin told them with gusto and enjoyment. A broad smile covered his face right through the recording and his eyes were shining. He was definitely enjoying himself.

Vishal and I left Mumbai delighted. We knew we had a stunning interview on tape. The only problem was reducing it to twenty-five minutes. That wasn't going to be easy because we wanted to keep every answer and it was impossible to decide which ones to drop.

Eventually—as had to happen—the job got done and the interview was reduced to the requisite time. But I still feel that what got left out was at least as good as what we retained. I'm confident Vishal would not disagree. If only the BBC had let us make a two-part episode rather than insist on sticking to one!

13

A HOP, SKIP AND JUMP—AND
A BOMB BLAST

My years with *Eyewitness* ended in 1997. What followed was an interesting hop, skip and jump between different jobs before I formed my company Infotainment Television Private Limited with my old school friend Analjit Singh as my sleeping business partner.

The first hop, so to speak, was a year with Markand Adhikari's Sri Adhikari Brothers. I skipped out of there within a brief year and jumped at an opportunity to join Ronnie Screwvala's United Television (UTV).

It was during my three years at UTV that most of the programmes that I came to be identified with began or started to attract attention. The list includes *HARDtalk India* and *Face to Face* for the BBC, *We The People* for Star TV (incidentally, Barkha Dutt 'stole' that title after we finished this particular series) as well as *Line of Fire* and *Court Martial* for SAB TV. To be honest, the last two programmes started while I was with Markand Adhikari but reached their acme after I left him.

The famous Kapil Dev interview when he cried like a baby happened whilst I was with Ronnie's company. Another memorable one during my time there was with General Pervez Musharraf. It achieved an extraordinary level of attention, both because of its content and timing.

The Musharraf interview happened just four months after the coup of 1997 when the general dismissed the Nawaz Sharif government and took charge himself. More importantly, it was just weeks after the hijack of IC-814, known popularly as the Kandahar hijack. An Indian aeroplane travelling from Kathmandu to Delhi was hijacked by terrorists and flown to Kandahar, Afghanistan, and forcibly held there. To end the ensuing hostage crisis, the Indian government was forced to release three Pakistani terrorists in its custody who were taken to Kandahar by then external affairs minister, Jaswant Singh.

'I want to interview Gen. Musharraf,' I said to Ashraf Qazi one morning. 'He could be a very badly misunderstood man and, therefore, it would surely be in his interest to speak directly to the Indian people and let them see and judge him for what he really is. Don't you agree?'

Ashraf didn't completely fall for this gambit; he was too astute for that. However, he could see the utility of an interview with a military dictator that might help improve the latter's image, particularly just after the Kandahar hijack.

It was in early February while I was on a visit to Mumbai that Ashraf rang to say that the interview had been fixed. 'You have to leave on Friday. The interview is on Saturday. Fortunately, there is a flight that day to Lahore with an easy connection to Islamabad.'

This was good news, but the problem was that it was already Wednesday. Gen. Musharraf was giving me just forty-eight hours' notice to research, prepare and travel.

'Karan,' Ashraf replied, when I complained about the shortage of time, 'you wanted an interview and you've got it. You're the first

Indian to be given this opportunity. Grab it now or you'll lose it forever.'

I didn't need further convincing. I knew this was an opportunity I couldn't let slip out of my grasp.

Expectedly, it was a quarrelsome, even aggressive interview. After the hijack, Musharraf wasn't popular in India. More importantly, as a journalist from the world's largest democracy, I could hardly be soft on a military dictator who had overthrown Pakistan's most recent attempt at civilian government. Finally, to ensure that Doordarshan would show the finished product—and that was one of the paradoxes of this interview; it was to be shown on India's national television and not on a private channel—it had to be tough. Any weakness on my part would have ensured Doordarshan would refuse to broadcast it.

So, as an Indian interviewer, my first objective was to get him to accept that he was a military dictator and that his claim to be restoring democracy was codswallop. The other was to talk to him about how his actions—or lack of them—were the real problem in Indo–Pakistan relations.

As you can imagine, this was not the sort of task that would endear an interviewer to the interviewee and I must admit there was a certain apprehension in my heart. I wasn't scared or worried, but I felt that things might not go well. After all, you can't sit in a man's drawing room and call him a tanashah, a dictator, to his face and not annoy or, at least, upset him. When that would inevitably happen, the atmosphere, equally inexorably, would turn frosty.

Well, I did my bit. I called the general a dictator. I told him that in Indian eyes, his sincerity and credibility were utterly suspect and I claimed to have discovered the contradictions that bedevilled him. He was an army chief who had overthrown an elected prime minister in the name of democracy, yet wanted his protestations to be taken at face value even though he was not prepared to do very much to prove his credentials. As I put it to him, what could be more bizarre than that?

The general simply smiled. In fact, it wasn't long before I noticed that he was unperturbed. Of course, he defended himself, always fluently, often ably and even nodded in agreement with some of the comments I made. By taking my criticism on the chin and showing no anger, he cleverly defused the situation.

During the commercial break, instinctively feeling that I needed to make small talk to keep our communication going, I complimented the general on his tie. I hadn't expected any response, leave aside the one I got.

'Do you really like it?' he asked, a smile lighting up his face and his voice revealing the same innocent pleasure that you or I feel when someone admires our clothes.

'Yes I do,' I said. 'It's very attractive.'

Then the interview restarted. The second half was about Kashmir, which means the disagreements were sharper and the potential for acrimony greater. Half an hour later, when it ended, the tie was the last thing on my mind. My thoughts were on making a polite but fast getaway.

'I'd like you to have this,' General Musharraf suddenly said, undoing his tie. 'Please let me give it to you.'

'Sir, sir, sir,' I stammered. 'That was only an innocent remark. I wasn't hinting or anything.'

'I know,' he replied. 'It's my gesture of conciliation to you.'

'Thank you,' I said, still shaken. Then, looking at the gold tiepin and chain now idly dangling on his shirt, I added with a laugh, 'I should have admired the gold chain. Maybe you would have given that to me as well.'

The general roared.

145

'Haan,' he said. '*Aur agar aap ko jootein pasand aayi ho toh woh bhi mil jaatein* (And if you liked my shoes you would have got those as well)!'

In a flash the tension evaporated and the mood was full of bonhomie. The spontaneous gesture of gifting his tie had brought about a sea change. I wasn't the only person who felt it. My colleagues who had come with me were equally aware of the altered atmosphere and the fact that General Musharraf deserved credit for it. Their verdict said it all: '*Banda sahi hai. Bura nahin. Dil ka saaf hai* (He's not bad. A good-hearted man).'

There's one little story left to tell. It's about how Doordarshan was persuaded to telecast the interview. After Kargil and the Kandahar hijack, Musharraf was not a man Doordarshan wanted to promote. Yet, he was undoubtedly in the news and also controversial. So when I had approached the channel's chief executive officer prior to the interview, he agreed to show it in principle, provided the content justified a Doordarshan broadcast. That was the catch.

My next step was to contact Brajesh Mishra, who at the time was Atal Bihari Vajpayee's principal secretary and national security adviser. I asked if I could get an off-the-record briefing before the interview. He agreed and when I turned up I took along the questions I intended to put to General Musharraf. I wanted Mishra to approve them. If he did, that would be the first indication that I was on the right lines. It would also greatly help with Doordarshan.

Fortunately, Mishra liked what he saw. More unexpectedly, he also took to me. He asked me to get in touch as soon as I was back and offered to ensure that Doordarshan would broadcast the interview, provided I stuck to the questions I had shown him.

'No one can predict what Musharraf will say and I doubt if he's going to crumble in front of you,' he said. 'But if the questions are tough and asked with determination, it will show an Indian audience that this Pakistani dictator has been properly questioned. That's the sort of message this government would be happy with.'

Mishra liked the final interview when he saw an advance video copy of it. He also loved the stories I had come back with.

'Now we've got to be clever about this,' he said. 'You're going to face a lot of opposition and we have to tackle it before it hits us.'

I thought I understood what Mishra was saying but wasn't certain, so I kept quiet. Anyway, he had not finished.

'You're saying that Doordarshan plans to show it in three or four days' time, provided they get the necessary clearance from the government. Is that right?' he continued.

'Yes. But that clearance is the problem. Can you help me?'

'Well, the first thing to do,' Mishra said, 'is to get one or two papers to publish that Doordarshan will air this interview on whatever the target date is. Do you have an editor who is a friend who can arrange this?'

It didn't take me long to work out that Mishra's intention was to force the government's hand. Once it became widely known that Doordarshan intended to broadcast an interview with Gen. Musharraf, it would be that much more difficult to deny clearance. In those circumstances doing so would seem like censorship.

My recourse was to contact M.K. Razdan, then editor-in-chief of the Press Trust of India (PTI) and a good and supportive friend. During my *Eyewitness* years PTI, under his direction, had done more than anyone else to publicize our stories and help our programme establish its name.

I decided to level with Razdan and tell him the truth. Experienced journalist that he is, he laughed. He knew at once that this was a game that journalists and sometimes even politicians play. PTI immediately put out a little story that Doodarshan would carry an exclusive one-hour interview with Gen. Musharraf which, luckily, a couple of papers picked up the next day. One of them, if I recall correctly, was *The Indian Express*. It carried the article on the front page.

However, I still hadn't got the necessary clearance for broadcast. As the last few days rolled by, we were left with just hours before the scheduled telecast. If the clearance didn't happen by then, Mishra's tactics could actually leave us considerably embarrassed because now we would have to explain both why the interview wasn't broadcast and how the news about it had been leaked. So, instead of forcing the government's hand, we would end up incurring its wrath.

If my memory is correct, the broadcast was scheduled for 8 p.m. In the meantime, the interview had been seen by the army chief as well as External Affairs Minister Jaswant Singh. But I had no idea whether they approved or disapproved of it.

I kept trying to ring Brajesh Mishra but was unable to get through. His secretary was like a wall that I couldn't get past. I left several messages but got no response.

By 6 p.m. I was convinced that in this instance, no news was bad news. Then suddenly, the phone rang. It was Brajesh Mishra. He was clearly chuckling. I could tell he was in a good mood.

'What time is your interview scheduled for broadcast?' he began. But he didn't wait for my answer. 'If it's still 8 o'clock, that gives me enough time to get home and watch it with a drink. So I just thought I would ring and confirm that nothing has changed.'

This was Mishra's way of saying that he had got the clearance and the interview was on. He was fond of passing on messages in this elliptical fashion. I also thought he was rather pleased he had kept me in tension right to the bitter end.

Years later, when I got to know him well and we would dine with each other, he told me that Jaswant Singh had been against the telecast. In fact, Jaswant directly rang Prime Minister Vajpayee to say so. Mishra saw this as a bit of a challenge and made a special effort to persuade Vajpayee that Jaswant's advice was mistaken. I suspect the rivalry between Mishra and Jaswant made certain that the former tried every means to ensure that the interview he was backing was shown. Perhaps if Jaswant had not made his opposition so obviously known, Mishra's exertions on my behalf would have been a lot less!

In the years that followed the Musharraf interview, I did several more with the general. In fact, a two-part interview with him launched *Devil's Advocate* in 2006. The astonishing thing is, though he was a dictator and now wants to be seen as a democrat, he has never hesitated to answer difficult questions and even seems to enjoy tackling them. Handling the media is definitely one of his strengths. Some of his civilian successors could learn from him.

∾

The other memorable incident from these years—if memorable is the appropriate word—was that I was one of the victims of a Tamil Tiger terrorist bomb attack in Colombo, Sri Lanka. It happened more than twenty years ago on 15 October 1997. Not surprisingly, my memory of the full story is weak, if not also inaccurate. Yet, the trauma of the experience and the injuries it left behind are still very much with me.

The only way I can relate what happened is to delve back into the piece I wrote for the *Hindustan Times* on my return. Called 'A Miraculous Escape', it recounts the details of what happened although, like any column, it's a touch embellished. Here's an updated version of the story I told then:

Like any other journalist I'm always on the lookout for a good story. The problem comes when instead of being the sutradhar, you end up the subject. Suddenly, your emotions get entangled with the chronology and no detail seems too small

149

or insignificant to leave out. No wonder journos who write about themselves end up [becoming] crashing bores.

Yet having found myself in the middle of a bomb blast that made headlines across the globe, the desire to talk about it—perhaps even gloat—is irresistible. After all, I was an eyewitness and I did live through what happened. And now that it's over—and I can see how providential my escape was—I can't help thanking God I'm still around.

There can be no doubt that Sri Lanka is a troubled island. But the one thing I hadn't expected was a bomb, although in retrospect there certainly were hints I should have paid more thoughtful attention to. They started at 7 a.m. Fitfully asleep in a corner room on the thirteenth floor of the Colombo Hilton, I awoke to what sounded like gunfire. Yet so powerful is the urge to rationalize that I immediately decided the noise was fireworks, the fifteenth being a national holiday in this Buddhist country.

No more than five minutes would have lapsed before curiosity and the fact that the Hilton overlooks President Kumaratunga's office started to disturb my sangfroid. Telephoning the reception, I enquired if a coup d'état was in progress. I meant it as a facetious joke. The reply I got was deadly serious. 'It's unauthorized firing, sir. Please stay in your room, don't look out of the windows and keep the curtains drawn.'

Minutes later it happened. It was the loudest noise I've ever heard. A bomb had gone off thirteen floors below.

Thereafter, things happened so fast—and fear, I suppose, can generate such speed—that what followed must have occurred in a trice. I can remember the huge bay windows flying towards me but I cannot recall shooting out of bed and darting out of the room.

My next memory is in the corridor outside, staring at my shredded pyjamas. The waistband and a dangling cord was all that was left. Perhaps the pyjama top survived but if it did, I don't remember noticing. The floor around me and the whole of the room I had left was buried in broken glass, crushed plaster and twisted metal.

Stunned hotel guests began to emerge from their rooms. Their faces were covered with debris and dust, broken by trickles of blood, turning at times into little streams and occasionally torrents. We stared at each other, the enormity of our recent experience beginning to sink in when we saw it on each other's faces or bodies. 'Are you okay? You're bleeding pretty badly.' Invariably the reply was, 'So are you.'

For a while we just stood around. Shock, at first, is like paralysis. You don't know what to do. Although there was constant firing outside, to us, after the big blast, it seemed strangely silent. Then an instinct for survival took over. Was the hotel structure safe? Or would it start capsizing from the top downwards? And where was everyone else?

Someone found the stairs and single-file, silently but with incredible concentration, we descended. Smoke and dust were rising from the bottom whilst a burst water-main on top provided a Niagara-like backdrop.

'Mind your shoes,' came a voice from the vanguard.

'What shoes? I don't have any.'

'Don't worry, you'll have bandages instead pretty soon.'

We headed for the hotel kitchens on the ground floor. I suppose, behind their thick metal doors, which opened on to the devastated and deserted lobby, it felt safe. But the phones were dead. I'm not sure how long we were there, perhaps thirty minutes, maybe even an hour and a half.

Outside, the Sri Lankan army and the Liberation Tigers of Tamil Eelam (LTTE) were battling it out. Inside, we started taking stock. The comparatively less injured organized search parties for unaccounted friends. Most of the crew from various incoming airlines, who had checked in the night before, were missing. A few people could not locate business colleagues. One particularly distraught lady could not find her husband.

Meanwhile, the hotel chefs turned to first aid. Dishcloths, tea towels, even napkins were torn and used as bandages and tourniquets, the kitchen Savlon was carefully shared, whilst the few available tablets of paracetamol were reserved for those whose injuries were most appalling to behold.

And there were some horrific ones. One hotel employee had a six-inch shard of glass buried inside his shoulder blade. A middle-aged European was holding his right thigh with his hands but it kept slipping through his fingers and falling out. Yet I don't recall anyone crying or even wincing. I suppose stage two of shock is when you know you are injured but can't feel the pain.

If there was fear, it was mostly well hidden. However, we were really scared when the Sri Lankan army came to our rescue. In their panic, the soldiers were shouting, their behaviour aggressive. With hands raised above our heads, we were marched out. Overzealous soldiers were pushing those at the back, frequently prodding with their guns.

For many who had expected sympathy and understanding, this proved too much. Silently and helplessly they started to weep. Some simply squatted where they were and refused to move. It wasn't defiance, nor was it hesitation. Just a sudden collapse of will. Stage three of shock hits you when it's effectively all over. With relief comes a surge of suppressed emotions.

My 'heroes' on that black Wednesday were women. First there was a sixty-year-old Dutchwoman, Karin Stevens, who had befriended me in the kitchens. Although herself unhurt and no doubt anxious to get away, she insisted on accompanying me to the hospital. Even in the operating theatre, my bloodied shoes in her hands, she would not leave my side.

'I've got a big bottle of whisky in my box,' she whispered in my ear reassuringly. 'After this is over we're going to have a drink together.' Unfortunately, we never did but wherever you are, Karin—and even if you never read this—thank you very much.

My other heroine was the Indian charge d'affaires's wife. Her husband sent his bulletproof jeep and bodyguards to escort me from the hospital to their home. I arrived in a blood-splattered hotel gown, my legs and hands in bandages, my forehead stuck with plaster. At 11 o'clock on a holiday morning, I wasn't exactly a pretty sight for a housewife to behold. But Mrs Prakash—I never got to know her first name—took me in her arms.

In minutes she was sponging and towelling me, peeling-off caked blood and gently cleaning my glass-cut abrasions. 'Remember I'm a mother,' she chided firmly but kindly as my cheeks reddened with embarrassment. 'Let's clean you up and get you into fresh clothes and you'll feel a lot better.' How right she was.

It's now been two decades, but I can still recall the blast as if it happened seconds ago. Fortunately, my memories of Karin and Mrs Prakash are equally strong.

But there are also other recollections that occasionally come to mind. One of the most reassuring is of the Sri Lankan surgeon who had stitched a cut tendon on my left index finger. At the time, too scared to look, I had turned my head the other way. 'Will I die, doctor?' I'd asked.

'Certainly not in my hands,' he shot back. 'And before you do, this finger will be good enough to poke into many more trouble spots!'

14

DISILLUSIONMENT WITH AMAL CLOONEY AND BARACK OBAMA

Have you noticed how the people you are eager to meet often prove to be disappointing? Perhaps anticipation builds up huge expectations but rather than their perceived star qualities, it's their faults and flaws you notice. Consequently, heroes end up with feet of clay.

In the last couple of years, I have experienced this on at least two prominent occasions. Each proved to be a huge disappointment. Though at the time the need for discretion kept my lips sealed, now I feel I can be more open. One reason for doing so—and there could be many others—is that the experiences I have to relate may feel familiar to several other people. My story could therefore strike a chord with you.

In March 2016 I was invited to moderate the gala finale of the India Today Conclave with Amal Clooney. The combination of a high-flying internationally acclaimed lawyer and the wife of one of Hollywood's leading stars was irresistible. I accepted with alacrity.

Now let me not mislead you. There's no doubt that Mrs Clooney is striking. Though painfully thin, she has presence. I wouldn't call her beautiful but she is undoubtedly attractive. There's something about her that makes you want to look again and again. At least initially, I couldn't keep my eyes off her.

Additionally, she is soft-spoken, charming and even coy. When she talks about George—and she does it only occasionally and quite reluctantly—there's a winning bashfulness. It's almost as if she can't believe he's her husband!

Sadly, there is also another side to Amal Clooney, a side that contradicts the freedom of speech she espouses. And it diminishes her.

Mrs Clooney's formal speech to the conclave was about freedom of speech. She spoke about her famous clients, former president Mohamed Nasheed of the Maldives; Mohamed Fadel Fahmy, Al Jazeera's former chief of bureau in Egypt who had been imprisoned for months; and Khadija Ismayilova, an Azerbaijani journalist who was then languishing in jail. Though she didn't say so, Amal Clooney emerged as the protector of their liberty and, perhaps, their best hope for justice. As she spoke, the audience warmed to this self-presentation.

Alas, how different was the reality hidden under the surface, which the audience was unaware of. Amal Clooney, though speaking to a conclave organized by a television channel, had forbidden the live broadcast of her speech as well as the question-and-answer session that followed. She also insisted that nothing could be broadcast afterwards without her clearance, which meant that she wanted the right to edit whatever she was asked or said.

In the end, nothing of her speech was broadcast and only approximately six minutes of her thirty-minute Q&A were permitted to be shown.

This was the extent to which Amal Clooney 'censored' the channel that hosted her. Of course, she had a contract that permitted this. So it was her prerogative to exercise these rights and the channel, no doubt, had been shortsighted in agreeing to such terms. But the incongruity of a human rights lawyer who champions freedom of speech insisting on rigidly restricting the broadcast of what she said was, for me, more damaging than anything else.

The bizarre part is that if Mrs Clooney's speech and Q&A had been broadcast in full—live or afterwards—it would only have added to her image, because she handled both with considerable aplomb.

Now, instead of recalling with delight what is probably a once-in-a-lifetime experience, I feel disillusioned. I didn't know what to expect of her, but it certainly wasn't this. Who would have believed that Amal Clooney, of all people, would twist Voltaire's famous dictum into 'I will fight to the death to ensure you can't broadcast what I have said unless you let me edit it'?

I guess you could say that Amal Clooney preaches freedom of speech but, at least, in her own case, practises something closer to censorship.

If anything, the second time something similar happened was even more disillusioning. That's because it involved one of the world's brightest political stars. Amal Clooney is well-known, but this guest occupies a much higher level of the stratosphere, almost entirely on his own. He is someone the world admires and he's uniformly regarded as one of the best orators of our time. He is also thought of as one of the best former heads of government, good-looking and incredibly charming. And if you haven't guessed whom I'm referring to, the answer is Barack Obama.

Former president Obama was the key and most sought-after guest at the Hindustan Times Leadership Summit in December 2017.

News that he was to attend became known a few months earlier and with every passing day the frisson of excitement grew more palpable. The Indian capital was increasingly on edge. Everyone was waiting for Obama's arrival and the session with him. At least two channels—CNN-News18 in India and Channel News Asia in Singapore—had promised to broadcast it live. Thousands were telephoning the *Hindustan Times* or asking their friends for passes to attend. Everyone wanted to be present.

Some four weeks before D-day, I suddenly got a call from the chairperson and editorial director of the *Hindustan Times*, Shobhana Bhartia, my former boss who has remained a good friend.

'Karan,' Shobhana began, 'can I come and see you?'

'Of course,' I said, somewhat surprised. Shobhana had never asked to see me before and I couldn't understand why she felt the need to do so now. 'But what's the problem? What's happened?'

'I want to ask you for a favour.'

'But you don't have to come to my office to do that!' I replied, somewhat flabbergasted. 'You can ask over the phone and I would be happy to help in any way I can.'

Only Shobhana knew where our conversation was heading. I was clearly flummoxed which, perhaps, is why she suddenly started giggling. When she does, she sounds like an innocent schoolgirl. You would never believe she's actually sixty years old.

'You know I've got Barack Obama coming for the Leadership Summit this year. I wondered if you would moderate the session with him?'

'Do you call that asking for a favour?' I responded. This time the incredulity in my voice was only too apparent. To use a colloquialism, I was gobsmacked.

Shobhana had perhaps the most important former politician in the world coming for her summit and she was offering me the opportunity—no, asking me—to chair the session with him. Every journalist in India would have jumped at this chance. For me, by then boycotted by Narendra Modi and his government, this was a heaven-sent opportunity to re-establish my credentials and cock a snook at the miserable-heartedness of the BJP.

'Of course I'll do it. I'm thrilled and honoured to accept.'

This time both of us started giggling and I suddenly felt as if I was back at school.

Preparations for the Obama session began almost immediately. However, this is also when the scales began to fall from my eyes. With every passing day, it became not just apparent but undeniable that Barack Obama is not an easy man to deal with. In fact, he is so protective of himself and so determined to avoid awkward and difficult moments that he has no hesitation in making demands that amount to censoring his interlocutors.

With three weeks still left for D-Day, I was told by the Hindustan Times Leadership Summit director, Anand Bhardwaj, that Obama wanted the questions he was likely to be asked in advance. Once upon a time, this used to be normal practice in India when local politicians were being interviewed. It was certainly the case in the early 1990s. But for the last decade or more, once Indian politicians had grown accustomed to television and tough interviews, this practice had fallen by the side. Now only a few make this request and, when they do, most of them know they are likely to be fobbed off with questions that probably will never be asked. So the majority don't bother.

Yet here was Obama, a former American president and one of the Western world's most important leaders, making demands I didn't believe Western politicians would ever ask of their own media.

I expressed my astonishment to Anand, but was told that the paper had agreed to Obama's request. In addition, Anand didn't seem to think it was such an extraordinary demand.

So I submitted an initial list of sixteen questions. This seemed to me more than adequate for the twenty minutes I would have to question Barack Obama. Even sixteen was probably six questions too many.

The format that had been decided for the session was a simple one. Barack Obama would first address the audience and his speech was expected to last for some forty minutes. This would be followed by a twenty-minute Q&A with me. The full session would last for an hour.

Within days of sending the questions, Anand Bhardwaj called to say that the Obama team wanted five dropped. It didn't take me long to discover that these five were the potentially difficult ones in the collection. But they also happened to be questions that either dealt directly with issues he had covered or decisions he had taken as president or with primary concerns for the Indian people.

'Why?' I asked Anand. 'On what grounds does he want these questions dropped?'

Anand seemed as perplexed as me. He certainly didn't have a clear, leave aside convincing, answer to offer on the Obama team's behalf.

'Does the Obama team realize that I'm asking the questions, and even if I agree to drop five questions now, what's to stop me bringing back a few at the session itself? And what will Obama do if that's what happens? Will he refuse to answer? Will he claim we had an agreement not to ask these questions? Or will he walk out?'

Anand laughed and so did I. If it wasn't such a demeaning situation for a former American president to place himself in, it would actually have been ridiculous. He was telling a journalist not to ask certain potentially awkward questions, which is as good as ensuring that any credible journalist would ask precisely those ones. This was like waving a sort of metamorphical red flag at a bull—it was bound to invite a challenging response, if not outright defiance.

Frankly, I gave Anand not just sufficient but repeated indications that I was determined to resurrect at least two, if not three, of the questions I had been told to drop. The reason was simple. They either referred to critical aspects of Obama's diplomacy with India or touched on issues of fundamental concern to an Indian audience.

In either event, the audience would have expected me to ask them. As a journalist, I felt I had a duty to do so. Furthermore, my amour propre would not let me act otherwise. I would have felt small and diminished if I had. But let me be honest. I also sensed that these questions, when asked, would add a lot of life to the Q&A with Obama. Depending on his answers, they could electrify the session and, perhaps, make for front-page headlines in all the newspapers the next morning. This was too much to ask any journalist to forego. I certainly wasn't going to be so self-denying.

The first question was to do with Obama's claim, made when he visited India as chief guest on Republic Day in 2015, that the resolution of the nuclear liability issue was 'a breakthrough understanding'. No one else believed that and certainly events have not borne out Obama's exaggerated description. Here's the precise question:

> The 2015 visit, when you came as chief guest on Republic Day, ended with an agreement resolving the nuclear liability issue which you called 'a breakthrough understanding'. In contrast, *The New York Times* said it was 'vague and inconclusive' and an attempt to kick the problem into the long grass. Given that nearly three years have passed and neither Westinghouse nor GE have taken meaningful steps to establish a nuclear plant in India, whose description was right? Yours or *The New York Times*'?

The other question I was determined to retain was about what Indians consider America's equivocation, or even two-facedness, over the terror India faces from certain groups in Pakistan. This is a concern that practically every Indian I know has. With a former American president as my interlocutor, I would have been foolish not to bring it up. Here's the question:

Now you once said: 'America can be India's best partner.' On another occasion you called India-US relations 'one of the defining partnerships of the twenty-first century'. And to be honest, both your predecessor and your successor have spoken in very similar terms. Yet many Indians feel that America differentiates between the terror groups based in Pakistan that target Afghanistan and, perhaps, the US, and those like LeT and Jaish that target India. How do you address this concern?

Alas, Obama didn't really answer either. Though he spoke at length, he deftly evaded answering. However, having decided to retain these two—and one other which I will come to later—I felt I had created an opportunity to weave in an interesting supplementary. It was to do with the American Navy SEALs operation that had eliminated Osama bin Laden in Pakistan's Abbottabad in 2011. Since Obama was the president at the time and this was an event that had captured the world's imagination—and left Pakistan squirming with embarrassment or smouldering with anger, depending upon your political viewpoint—it was hard not to bring it up. In fact, it was downright irresistible.

So, after questioning President Obama about America's two-tone attitude to terror, I asked: 'In 2011, American Navy SEALs flew undetected into Pakistan and eliminated Osama bin Laden. Was Pakistan hiding him and, therefore, complicit? Or unaware of his presence and, therefore, incompetent?'

If I recall his answer correctly, Barack Obama firmly said that his administration had no evidence that Pakistan was aware of Osama bin Laden's presence in Abbottabad. He then tantalizingly added, 'I'll leave it to you to characterize beyond what I just said.'

This was an opportunity I couldn't let slip. Given the way he phrased it, he was almost tempting me to draw my own conclusion and put it to him.

'So it was incompetence?' I asked. The former American president wouldn't say. He was determined not to be drawn further. All he did was smile.

By coincidence, I had posed the same question to former president Musharraf at a Hindustan Times Leadership Summit a couple of years earlier. When I asked him if Pakistan was either complicit or incompetent he'd said—with surprising candour but also not inconsiderable humour—that the truth was the ISI had fallen asleep!

'That's neglect, isn't it?' I had persisted.

But Musharraf wasn't going to agree. 'No, let's say the ISI fell asleep,' he said and smiled knowingly. 'But the ISI has the right to go to sleep occasionally.'

I repeated this story to Obama in front of the Hindustan Times audience and though he laughed, I still couldn't get him to say anything more.

However, the former president was particularly deft and also forthcoming while handling questions about Indian politicians he had known as prime ministers when he was president.

'A lot has been written about your relationship or friendship with Narendra Modi,' I said. 'At his invitation, you became the first American president to be chief guest on Republic Day, you did a joint radio broadcast and Prime Minister Modi frequently refers to you as my friend Barack. What's your opinion of Narendra Modi?'

Like any sound politician, Barack Obama had his antenna up. He instinctively sensed that he had to praise Narendra Modi but he also knew that in India's divided political environment, he needed to balance what he said by an equally fulsome reference to Manmohan Singh. And that's precisely what he did.

However, many in the audience and, at least, one or two of the newspapers the next morning, interpreted his balancing act as reluctance to praise only Modi. This, consequently, made for a few headlines.

The nice part was that I had more time to question Barack Obama than the twenty minutes in the original schedule. His prepared speech had barely lasted fifteen minutes. That was at least twenty, if not twenty-five minutes shorter than expected. My Q&A was the beneficiary. It now stretched for forty-five minutes.

This worked to both our advantage. It gave me time to bring in the questions I knew Obama did not want asked without dropping any that I sensed he was keen to speak about. In turn it gave him a chance to speak as he likes to, at considerable length. His answers were by no means short and were often not to the point. He likes to weave a lot of substance into his replies and he enjoys sounding cerebral or academic. Since he's an engaging if not riveting speaker, the length of his answers adds considerably to the spell he creates.

So by the time we came to the end of the hour, I felt I could get away with one more 'resurrected' question. This time it wasn't a serious one. It was an attempt at humour so that our conversation would end on a light-hearted note. My intention was to leave the audience laughing.

'Finally, President Obama,' I began, 'America is famous for two Donalds—Donald Duck and Donald Trump. Which one represents the real America?'

The audience got the joke at once and burst into laughter. We all expected a witty comeback from the former president. But that was not to be. Instead, he chose to sidestep the question and deliver a long homily on equality and the importance of treating people fairly.

Perhaps he didn't get the joke or, perhaps, he thought it wasn't appropriate for him to reply jocularly. But the answer he gave—though fabulously delivered—was inapt. It even felt strange. It seemed like a non sequitur.

Later I was told that the former president had found the question offensive. But for the life of me I'm not sure what offended him unless, of course, it's improper and inappropriate to joke with him or ask him to respond to one.

All of this means that my memories of meeting Barack Obama are a confusing, if not polarizing, mix of awe and delight alongside disappointment and disillusionment. There's no doubt that at one level he comes across as an inspiring, charming, informal and friendly celebrity. He's bewitching, though he keeps you at a distance, but that reserve, paradoxically, only enhances the attraction you feel. But on another level, it was deeply disillusioning to discover how he wanted to vet questions, strike out those he did not like and complain because a few had still been asked. It's not what I'd expected of him and it made me question whether the captivating image we all have is also carefully manufactured or as cosmetically created as his approach to the Q&A.

It didn't take me long to sense that the *Hindustan Times* was a little shaken, perhaps even somewhat upset, by the fact that Obama hadn't left covered in smiles. Though the paper is used to handling difficult politicians, this was a special summit and Obama a special guest. The fact that he had told Shobhana Bhartia, as she bid him farewell, that you can never be sure how a session with a journalist will go, made me feel that I needed to make amends. Not an apology; far from it. But I thought I should write about the Obama session for my 'Sunday Sentiments' column in the *Hindustan Times* in a way that, if he read it, might make him smile this time. My intention was to whip up a sweet taste at the end.

Nothing that I wrote was untruthful or even exaggerated, but I deliberately picked up on moments that might otherwise have got squeezed out and forgotten. I also wrote about them a bit like a silly schoolgirl with my head in the clouds! And I'm glad to say it worked. At least one senior member of the Obama team telephoned to thank me.

This is the piece that appeared forty-eight hours after the Obama session, on 1 December 2017:

In Mummy's heyday in the '20s and '30s, the opening line of one of the hit numbers of that period was: '*I've danced with a man, who's danced with a girl, who's danced with the Prince of Wales.*' This weekend I feel a bit like that!

On Friday I moderated the Hindustan Times Leadership Summit session with Barack Obama and discovered that beyond being a brilliant speaker and a very intelligent man, he's also truly special because of the little things he remembers and makes a point of speaking about. Grand politicians usually have no time for such niceties. Obama, who's amongst the greatest of them all, is different.

I was introduced to him before the formal session. A few people were invited for what was quaintly called 'a handshake reception'. Luckily, I was one of them.

Each of us got a chance to be photographed with Barack Obama. This is one of the chores celebrities are required to perform and usually do so with their impatience and irritation discernable. But not Barack Obama. He had a sentence or two for every one of the ninety people. He had never met any of us but he made every single person feel special.

'Oh dear,' he said, as we shook hands and he noticed I was wearing a tie. 'You're moderating the session and I've just realized I should have worn a tie as well. Is that okay? Or have I made a foolish mistake?'

Once the session got underway I discovered another side of this rather special man. There were a few questions he would have preferred not to be asked, but his response was to joke about that and then proceed to give a seemingly full answer until you discovered he had deflected the subject and spoken about something quite different.

I've interviewed several heads of government and you can see the lines on their face twitching or the steely look glazing their eyes as you probe a subject they don't feel comfortable with. That wasn't the case with Barack Obama. If anything, he would smile each time I trod on awkward territory. Once, perhaps, his eyebrows rose, but it was a gesture of comic exasperation which appealed to the audience.

The coup de grâce was when the mikes failed and Obama was caught halfway through a joke about cooking dal. To be stopped just before your punchline can be exasperating. But not for Barack Obama.

He took it with a smile and said: 'This sort of thing has happened so often I've got quite used to it. I've had the lights fail, members of the audience faint and even the stage collapse. What sort of experience have you had?'

Not as quick-witted as the former American president, I couldn't even make up an amusing story. So we chatted about Theresa May's misfortunes at the Conservative Party conference in September when a coughing fit overcame her and she barely finished her speech.

'Wasn't that awful?' Obama said. 'My heart went out. There's nothing worse than a politician all prepped to speak suddenly finding they can't get their voice out.' And he laughed silently.

It's unlikely any of us will meet Barack Obama again. Yet few will forget the enormous impact he made and I'm delighted I can tell stories about our conversation. The song from the '20s ends with the words 'Glory, glory, Hallelujah! I'm the luckiest of females!' Change the sex and that could be me!

15

THE WRATH OF RAM JETHMALANI

I guess I have a strange relationship with Ram Jethmalani. To begin with, he has always been very kind to me. He's never declined an interview. On one occasion when he was part of a discussion for a SAB TV programme which he had accepted without realizing he would be in Patiala at the time, he chartered a plane and flew back to Delhi at his own expense because he didn't want to ditch me. But at the same time, many of the interviews I have done with him have ended in 'quarrels'. He has walked out at least once and, I suspect, hasn't forgiven me for it. Yet, the paradox is that each time we've quarrelled, the interview has gone on to win an award. Two consecutive interviews done for *Devil's Advocate* won Singapore's Asian Television Award for Best Current Affairs Anchor of the Year. I'm certain it was the drama or spectacle of his wrath which convinced the jury that I had bearded the lion in his den!

The first *Devil's Advocate* interview happened in November 2006 and, to be honest, I was on very weak ground. Ram Jethmalani was defending Manu Sharma against the charge of killing Jessica Lal.

168

After Sharma's initial acquittal, the case had been reopened under media pressure and many of my colleagues were infuriated by Ram's decision to defend him.

In my 'Sunday Sentiments' column, I berated my colleagues who were visibly and, often, loudly angry that Mr Jethmalani had taken up Manu's case. I decided to defend his right to do so. This is what I wrote, and it went on to haunt me just days later:

My concern is simple. How can any credible journalist argue that Ram Jethmalani—or any other lawyer for that matter—should not defend Manu Sharma? No matter how you present this argument—and last week we saw many attempts to do so—I cannot understand the rationale for this position.

First, who a lawyer defends is a matter to be determined by his conscience. Friends and advisers may choose to influence him and, if they do, it's because he's granted them that right. But it's not a matter for journalists to opine on. Flip the situation and you'll see why. Would the same journalists accept Ram Jethmalani criticizing them for choosing to interview alleged terrorists or apparent criminals?

When Margaret Thatcher barred the British press from interviewing members of the IRA (Irish Republican Army) on the grounds that it gave them 'the oxygen of publicity', our entire fraternity rightly protested and condemned her decision. Surely that sword cuts both ways?

Second, in the eyes of the law—as opposed to the press—Manu Sharma is an innocent man. In fact, he stands acquitted by the lower court, although possibly wrongly so. Therefore, if that acquittal is to be appealed, it follows he has a right to defend himself. In turn that means he has a right to a lawyer and, ipso facto, the best he can get. Does it make sense for journalists to argue otherwise?

It's an irrefutable sine qua non of justice that every accused has the right to a defence and a lawyer to present it for him. Anything less would undermine the system of justice we believe in. In those circumstances the High Court might become a kangaroo court, the prosecution could degenerate into vendetta and the accused would transform into a victim. Is that what these journalists are seeking?

However, it's the third consequence of their argument that is possibly most embarrassing. It contradicts the very cause they've set out to champion. 'Justice for Jessica' is the campaign that has secured the retrial of Manu Sharma. Without this pressure from the press, it may never have been achieved. But if justice for Jessica is to be more than a semi-alliterative slogan, it cannot metamorphose into malice for Manu. Yet if journalists are to stop lawyers defending him, that, undoubtedly, is what it will become.

Last weekend, as I heard interviews and read articles on this subject, the subtext that underlay both was hard to ignore: 'We want justice for Jessica but without giving Manu Sharma the right to defend himself.' Once you strip the interviews of their passion and the articles are shorn off their clever phrases, this is the indefensible message left behind.

Perhaps the real concern is that a lawyer of Jethmalani's skill might succeed in saving Manu Sharma. Given that we're all 'convinced' of his guilt that would seem like a travesty of justice. Hence the opposition to Jethmalani taking up his case. But this is to place emotion ahead of justice.

The law permits Jethmalani to try every legitimate tactic to defend his client and if he succeeds so be it. That is the law and you can't complain just because the verdict doesn't suit you. It may prove there are infirmities that need to be plugged, that the system has holes, that justice is less than perfect, but you can't make it an excuse for short-circuiting procedure. Without due process the trial would be a lynching.

Remember, justice has to be seen to be done—and beyond all reasonable doubt. We all know what we want but the judges have to deliver it in a fair and transparent manner. Last week some of my colleagues forgot that.

However, for the *Devil's Advocate* interview I found myself switching positions in order to play 'devil's advocate' to Ram's stance. No longer was I criticizing his critics, I was criticizing him instead. The thrust of my questioning was to quarrel with his decision to defend Manu Sharma. 'How can you?' I asked. 'You're letting down all principle and morality,' I said. 'This is opportunism and you're only doing it for publicity,' I insisted. 'Finally, do you really believe the man is innocent?' I questioned, in a futile attempt to trip him up.

Ram would have been aware of what I had written. It had appeared just ten days before the interview was recorded. Yet, not once did he point out that I was arguing against my own published position. In retrospect, I'm grateful for that. Had he done so, I would have been stumped!

Not surprisingly the interview, almost from the start, became a quarrel. We initially talked over each other but it wasn't long before we were shouting. Not because he was genuinely angry or because I was being aggressive, but simply because that was the only way of being heard! In fact, for most of the crew the interview wasn't so much a discussion as one long interruption, where both sides were continuously interrupting each other.

At the end of the recording I suggested we do the interview all over again in the hope that the second version would be less quarrelsome and, therefore, easier for the audience to follow. Ram agreed. But the second attempt was no different to the first. If anything, because we knew each other's arguments, we were even faster at interrupting and each time that happened, it was done more loudly and more forcefully.

I could only laugh when it ended. Ram Jethmalani's response was even more good-natured.

'Let's have a whisky,' he said. 'We've both earned it and I need one badly!'

Nothing could have illustrated his good nature better than this generous gesture. There wasn't a hint of rancour. In fact, I would say he had enjoyed the whole process. Now that it was over, he wanted a drink with someone he still considered a friend. I readily accepted.

As I thought it would, the interview attracted a lot of attention. Long before it won the Asian Television Award, it became the subject of eager questioning. People would stop me at parties or, sometimes, in shops and want to talk about the interview. Was it really as quarrelsome as it seemed? Was Ram Jethmalani upset? Were we still on talking terms?

So often did this happen that I decided to write about it. I chose one particular instance as the best illustration of the curiosity the interview had provoked. The piece I did was for my 'Sunday Sentiments' column. It appeared in the first week of December 2006. Called 'Is an interview a game?' this is what it had to say:

'Excuse me Mr Thapar, but there's a question I'm dying to ask.'

I was at a wedding, standing on my own and feeling a little lost. So I welcomed the interruption. Turning around, I saw my interlocutor was a bubbly lady in her thirties in a striking strawberry-pink-and-gold sari. She seemed quite excited.

'Of course,' I replied encouragingly. 'Go right ahead.'

'How often do you find that after an interview your guests have stopped talking to you?'

I laughed nervously. To start with, I wasn't certain what she meant but decided it was intended as a compliment. However, I was also aware her comment appeared to suggest that I'm insufferably rude. I suppose it was her smile which made me overlook the innuendo.

'Why do you ask?' I hadn't meant to sound defensive but I fear I did. Still, since I don't think of myself as an ogre, it was a justified question.

It brought forth a loud cackle of laughter. I smiled sheepishly. It's rather embarrassing when people find your innocent remarks hilarious. Are they laughing with you or at you? I didn't know how to respond.

'I keep thinking of poor Mr Jethmalani. He was so angry with you.' At this point the lady in the pink sari started to convulse all over again. Soon her face was the colour of her clothes. Meanwhile my smile, by now frozen on my face, was starting to hurt. Worse, I was no longer sure which way our conversation was heading. So on top of everything else, I was also a little apprehensive.

'He must have kicked you out of the house.' Suddenly the laughter stopped and her face turned serious. In fact, it seemed severe. 'I don't think I would have blamed him if he had!'

'Actually, he offered me a glass of whisky.' It was my turn to smile. I managed a small one. After all I could feel my confidence crawling back. 'He asked if I would join him for a drink.'

'You mean the anger was put on?'

'No.' That should have been sufficient but I foolishly added a fuller explanation. 'First, I don't think he was angry. Perhaps irritated but not more. Secondly, Ram Jethmalani is a passionate and excitable person and always responds in a dramatic sort of way. And then, more than anything else, he's a gentleman. He never bears a grudge.'

However, my effort did not appease the good lady. She was not to be put off so easily. Her next line of attack was ready and it was delivered with aplomb. I was caught off guard.

'And does everyone forgive you so readily? You can't be that lucky every time.'

This time I was speechless. If the conversation had started with a certain unstated admiration of my style, there was now the clear suggestion that I overstep the limits of decency and rely on the large-heartedness of my interviewees to overlook this. I decided the time had come to explain why my interviews often become fractious.

'The point is this: if a question is worth asking, it's worth ensuring it gets an answer. So when a guest doesn't reply or actually evades I feel I have to persist. In turn that means a certain tension inevitably creeps in. Depending on how long it takes to break this impasse or how risible the guest, things can seem to get heated. But it's only momentary and it's only within the context of the interview.'

'Okay, that's your explanation. But do your guests see it the same way?' The lady had now crossed her hands in front of her chest. She was looking at me intently. I felt like a target.

'I think so.' But it was a weak reply. I needed to do better. 'You see, they realize I'm doing a job. And when they are being evasive or less than fulsome they're only protecting themselves. So I do think both sides understand the situation.'

'Hmmm.' A long pause followed as a slow smile started to crease her face. Behind it emerged a look of understanding, as if something important had suddenly dawned on her.

'So an interview is a game? Even an act? Is that what you mean?'

I was about to reply when I realized she wasn't finished. I held my peace.

'I suppose journalists and politicians are like cops and robbers. But in this case, who's the cop and who's the robber?'

If the first *Devil's Advocate* interview with him left our relationship—friendship?—intact, unfortunately, the second didn't end as felicitously. On that occasion the subject was Ram's decision to rejoin the BJP. After being forced out of Vajpayee's government and then breaking with the BJP in 2004, Ram had actually stood against Atal Bihari Vajpayee in the election of that year from Lucknow. At the time he had called Vajpayee's government 'a cesspool'. In fact, he had questioned whether the prime minister 'carries a sound mind in a sound body'. In a particularly low blow, he had added, 'I have a lot to say that will put this prime minister and his men in the dock.' Although he never revealed what was up his sleeve, he did repeatedly threaten to do so. Finally, he added: 'I am a friend of the prime minister. He is not my friend.'

So, in the circumstances, my line of questioning was clear and simple. After all that he had said, this decision in 2010 to rejoin the BJP was just an easy way of getting back into the Rajya Sabha. It was, as I put it, 'an act of gross opportunism devoid of all principle'.

On this occasion we didn't even get to the end of the interview's allotted twenty-two minutes. Roughly fifteen minutes in, Ram got up and left. I won't say he stormed out of the room because he's clearly too old for such a feat. But his anger was visible and he left in a very determined and resolute manner. He didn't return and I had to complete the interview by speaking directly to the camera to relate what I would have asked had the interview continued.

This incomplete interview, including my explanation for its abrupt ending, went on to win another Asian Television Award. I suspect it wasn't the quality of the interview that impressed the judges so much as the fact that the interviewee walked out. Juries are often impressed by such things.

Sadly, this time my relationship with Ram Jethmalani was damaged. He didn't forgive me and that, in turn, affected the way he viewed me. Although he gave me another interview some two years later, our relationship was never the same. The friendship and the trust had evaporated. No longer was I a journalist he would ring up. I was also struck off his dinner-party list.

Now when we meet, we smile and shake hands and he still calls me 'beta'. But we both know it's not the same. Once the ice is frozen over, it's hard to crack the surface and get back to where you were.

Which is why I prefer to remember Ram not by the two *Devil's Advocate* interviews but by the one I did during the days of *HARDtalk India*. It happened just after his forced resignation as law minister from the Vajpayee government. This was a particularly low moment in Ram's political career. If I recall correctly, he had made personal and uncomfortable allusions about the sitting chief justice which, many thought, were unacceptable from the law minister. That was enough to precipitate the resignation.

Every journalist wanted to interview Ram to get his side of the story. I was lucky and managed to convince him to give me his first. But the truth is, it wasn't I who sealed it so much as the fact that the interview was for the BBC.

It was when I dropped into Ram's Rajaji Marg residence to discuss the interview and fix the date that he surprised me by his behaviour. He began to tell me his side of the story. Getting into his stride, he pulled out his personal file and rapidly pointed out several letters and documents that proved his case. These, I realized, were critical.

'Can I borrow your file?' I suddenly asked. 'I'd like to go through these documents because then I can raise them in the interview and help you make your case.'

I was, in effect, asking Ram to trust me. Once I had his file he knew—and, for my part, I felt sure of this—there would also be things I could use against him. Far from helping, this could trip him up. But Ram Jethmalani is a trusting person and a warm-hearted one too. He took me at my word and gave me the file.

'You can have it, beta, but please treat it carefully.' And then he laughed. His eyes twinkled. 'Who knows what you'll find and how you'll use it. I'll probably regret giving you this file. But today, it's yours.'

We agreed to do the interview the following morning, which gave me the whole night to read the file and see what I could find.

All of this happened in July 2000 and that's so far back in time that I cannot recall the details clearly. What I do remember, however— and Ashok Upadhyay, my producer at the time, has confirmed it—is that we found a lot of stuff in Ram Jethmalani's file that we were able to use against him. What he had laughingly feared thus came to pass. I had borrowed the file to help him corroborate his position but used it, instead, to undermine his arguments.

I clearly recall the feeling of apprehension when the interview ended. Would Ram be upset? For sure he would know that I had not lived up to my promise. I had made good use of the file, but not in a way that would help him. The blunt truth is I had been selfish and all the advantage had accrued to me.

'Well, beta,' he said as the interview ended. He was smiling. It wasn't put on. 'You were in great form and you used that file to good effect.'

'Do you regret giving it to me?' I asked. It's not the sort of thing I've said before, when I've misled someone into doing something, but this time it just popped out of my mouth.

'Not at all,' he said. 'You see, you might have found a few useful points but you forget that I was always aware of them. Listen to the interview carefully and I have answers for each of the things you brought up. Now it's for the audience to decide what they believe. And isn't that what this is meant to be all about?'

To my delight, but also my surprise, Ram Jethmalani left in good humour. He had the file firmly tucked under his arm. More importantly, this was the start of a trusting relationship between a politician and a journalist that continued for a decade until the second *Devil's Advocate* interview brought it to an end.

16

AN ACRIMONIOUS INTERVIEW
WITH AMMA

It seems to me that there are two interviews I'm best known for. Both are political and ended on an acrimonious note. It's the underlying tension in them that, I believe, has caught everyone's attention. So, not surprisingly, both are frequently repeated. Indeed, at times they seem to have an independent life of their own on YouTube.

The first is the 2007 interview with Narendra Modi where he walked out after roughly three minutes. The second is an even older interview with J. Jayalalithaa, recorded in October 2004. She stayed the full course. But then, she left in a huff. This interview was much repeated when she died in December 2016, oddly enough, as a tribute to her. It showed her as a fiery lady and, therefore, revealed the tough metal she was made of. Let me start with this one.

The truth is, the Jayalalithaa interview rippled with tension from its very start. It ran through the conversation like an electric current.

Her manner and the increasingly cold and angry look on her face only added to the impact that made.

Which, no doubt, is why I've been repeatedly questioned about this interview. Most people suspect there's a story behind it, waiting to be told. And there is. I've hinted at it in my columns but never told it in full. Now, fourteen years later, I can be more forthcoming.

So let's start at the beginning. It took a lot of effort to secure the Jayalalithaa interview. If I'm not mistaken, it took years of trying before I succeeded. En route there was even a false start, an interview that I thought was fixed but which never happened.

When she did finally agree, it was on the condition that I submit my questions in advance. I protested that this was not the proper thing to request of a journalist. On the other hand, I was well aware that Jayalalithaa was not the first politician to make such a request. Several others had as well. In their cases, I had fobbed them off either with obvious questions that could easily have been predicted or false questions which I had no intention of ever asking. So I decided to do the same with her.

Mercifully, that did the trick. A date was fixed and when I conveyed the news to the BBC—their programme *HARDtalk India* would air the interview—they were particularly pleased. There's something about Jayalalithaa that makes everyone consider her special. The BBC was no exception.

The phone rang the night before I was to leave for Chennai. It was from the Tamil Nadu chief minister's office. My heart sank. Normally, such last-minute calls are harbingers of bad news.

'Sir,' said a placatory voice, a touch too eager to be the messenger of ill-tidings. 'Madam would like to start tomorrow's interview at 1.30 instead of 2.'

It was an unexceptional request. Though I breathed an audible sigh of relief, I still asked why.

'It's auspicious, sir.'

Determined not to let any impediment derail the interview, I readily agreed. Three years earlier, when Jayalalithaa had first accepted, a Supreme Court judgment unseating her torpedoed my plans. This time, when after much persuading she had said yes again, I was on tenterhooks.

Of all the people I had ever wanted to interview, Jayalalithaa was almost at the top of the list. She intrigued me. Her convent accent, sangfroid, deliberate manner and glide-like walk were captivating. She was so cultivated, so carefully put together, she seemed unreal.

I was therefore both nervous and excited as I entered Fort St George in Chennai. The silent army of faceless civil servants, beavering like ants, added to my tension. 'Madam' wasn't present but her presence was everywhere. The atmosphere was heavy with expectation and foreboding.

It was only the freezing cold temperature that prevented those of us waiting from swooning or going into a trance. I've never been in a colder room. My teeth were chattering, or they would have been if I hadn't kept talking. The thermostat was set at 18°C but the actual temperature was way below that.

Alas, the astrological calculations that had determined the interview hour proved false. Perhaps the stars were misinterpreted, for their augury went awry. Instead, Sod's Law took over. Put simply, that means everything that can go wrong will. And it did.

The trouble began with something as silly as flowers. Jayalalithaa had asked for some to be placed on the interview table. So a vast arrangement that stretched from end to end was readied. I balked and refused to allow this huge display to obstruct my view. Instead, I placed them on a stool by her side.

What I did not know was that the flowers were not intended for their beauty. Jayalalithaa wanted to hide her notes behind them. In their absence, the papers she carried became visible and, as the interview proceeded, I could see her flicking through them. From time to time, she even seemed to look down and read.

I suppose my mistake was to point this out. I don't know why I did it. Other interviewees have consulted papers before, although perhaps not so obviously or frequently. But on this occasion it slipped out of my mouth. Her reaction was instantaneous.

'I'm not reading,' she shot back angrily. 'I am looking at you straight in the eye. I look at everyone straight in the eye.'

In fact, the truth is that the interview got off to a bad start well before this happened. The problem began at its outset. The fault was undoubtedly my first question.

'Chief Minister, let's start with your image,' I began. 'For the last three years the press has at different times portrayed you as undemocratic, unreliable, irresponsible, irrational and even vengeful. Are you misunderstood or can you accept you have made errors and mistakes?'

Her reply was terse. It was a clear hint of what was to follow. 'I'm not irresponsible at all. That's totally removed from the truth. Yes, I'm misunderstood. As for all these other tags, that is because the media has been against me, not just for the past few years but ever since I came to politics.'

I had intended to attract attention with this question. Unfortunately, to Jayalalithaa, it probably felt like a personal attack. Yet it was clearly justified and, undoubtedly, needed to be asked because it touched on a key concern about her.

I should have been forewarned by the cold steel in her voice, but interviewers sometimes fail to sense what is obvious to others. Anyway, I had a set of questions and was determined to carry on.

'All right, let's explore some of the developments that have led to this image. Less than a week after your party failed to win a single seat at the national elections, you reversed a series of decisions taken in the last three years. Were you courting cheap populism or admitting to a mistake?'

Once again, she was hard as nails in her response. 'The changes made in May 2004 were termed by the media as rollbacks and they made it seem [as if] these were done in the wake of the parliamentary election results. That is not so. What I was attempting was a major recalibration of the process of structural adjustment ... I inherited a whole pile of unpaid bills. The fiscal balance had to be restored and this needed structural changes.'

This was another cue to rein myself in but now, I guess, I was turning defiant. I was determined to continue in the same vein. 'And what about the withdrawal of defamation cases against the media and the cancellation of punishment and disciplinary action against government servants for going on strike last year? They seemed arbitrary and unjustified then and they seem the same now.'

'The media is biased against me because I'm a self-made woman,' she replied. 'Politics has for long been a male bastion. The media picks on me because I don't have a family background like other female leaders of South Asia. Look at Indira Gandhi, Sirimavo Bandaranaike, Benazir Bhutto, Sheikh Hasina. They were all someone's daughter or wife. I have no such background. I'm a self-made woman.'

I heard out her answer and it's not that I was unconvinced by it. But I had set myself on a particular course and was determined to get to the end before I moved to another subject. So regardless of what she said, I wanted to carry on as planned.

'But do responsible chief ministers perform such spectacular U-turns?'

Now Jayalalithaa's response was not just terse and cold, you could almost feel the anger that underlay it. In turn, I knew I had a challenge on my hands. Part of me was apprehensive. You don't really take on a woman like Jayalalithaa without feeling a little nervous. But another part of me was determined to continue. This was a test not just of my journalism but also my courage. So, though it was time to change subjects, I was determined to stay on the attack.

I next raised the manner in which she had arrested her political adversary M. Karunanidhi. It had happened just over three years earlier. At the time he was seventy-seven and a former chief minister of fourteen years' standing.

'You arrested your predecessor at 2 in the morning on a Saturday, although the FIR against him had only been filed the day before. And then he was taken kicking and screaming to jail. Why was it done in this high-handed fashion?'

In fact, sections of the press had concluded that this was Jayalalithaa's revenge for the fact that Karunanidhi had arrested her after she lost power in 1996. They called it vengeance.

Once again, Jayalalithaa was incandescent. Her fury was all too visible.

'The DMK government foisted cases against me and threw me into jail. I languished in jail for twenty-eight days for a case in which I was ultimately acquitted. When Karunanidhi did this, the media gave him kudos, portraying it as the triumph of good over evil. When I became chief minister, Mr Karunanidhi was arrested in a corruption case. At the time his family channel, Sun TV, played a big hoax, putting out very cleverly edited footage. It was not vengeance. I do not regret it at all.'

Once again, changing subjects, I decided to put to her the zigzag way in which she had switched political alliances over the last six years. This was something that everyone was particularly aware of in 2004.

'Let's turn to what they call your unreliability. You fought the '98 elections opposed to Sonia, you fought the '99 elections as her ally, by 2003 you had changed sides again and now, after the Congress has won, you're claiming there is nothing personal about it. You seem to change your mind every time the mood in the country alters.'

This time Jayalalithaa refused to answer and she was adamant about it. 'I don't want to discuss Sonia Gandhi in this interview. I have a choice to pick and choose the questions I want to answer. I don't have to answer every question you put to me. I don't wish to discuss Mrs Sonia Gandhi.'

Yet again, I had a follow-up question ready, regardless of what Jayalalithaa's answer would be. Of course, I heard her reply but I was unwilling to be silenced or deflected.

'Do you know what the press says? They say you turned against Sonia Gandhi in 2003 to ingratiate yourself with the BJP and now you are reversing your decision to ingratiate yourself with the Congress.'

But it made no impact. She continued to refuse to answer. 'If you have any other questions you may put them. I have already told you I don't wish to answer this question.'

Thereafter, things only got worse. I questioned Jayalalithaa about her ministers who habitually prostrate before her and press accusations that she is dictatorial. With each change of subject her smile became more forced, her voice steelier and her irritation more obvious. 'I'm sorry I agreed to this interview,' she said and meant it.

But it was when I turned to her belief in astrology and numerology that I sensed I had gone too far. 'Who said that I believe in astrology and numerology?' she retorted, her eyes ablaze. 'You say it. People in the media say it. What is the proof you have of that?'

It was at this point that I belatedly realized the interview was going terribly wrong. In fact, disastrously so. In desperation, I tried to claw things back. With minutes to go I said, 'You are a very tough person, chief minister.' I meant it as praise but the comment backfired.

'People like you have made me so,' was her blunt reply.

I felt disheartened. Events have a way of taking over and determining their own outcome. This was happening before my eyes. It was happening to me! Finally, in the last dying seconds, as I thanked her, I stretched out my hand and added, 'Chief minister, a pleasure talking to you.'

For a moment she stared back implacably. 'I must say it wasn't a pleasure talking to you. Namaste.' She rebuffed my proffered hand, unclipped and banged down the mike, and sailed out of the room.

'Amma,' I wanted to shout, 'you've misunderstood me.' But it was too late.

In hindsight this may sound odd, but the truth is, at the time Ashok Upadhyay, my producer, and I were stunned by the way the interview had gone. We had expected it to go badly but not end the way it had.

After Jayalalithaa walked out in clear and obvious anger, the atmosphere froze. Every single official of the Tamil Nadu government left the room immediately. Suddenly, the crew, Ashok and I were on our own.

We instinctively felt we should pack up and leave as quickly as possible. We felt uncomfortable. Actually, we were on edge.

Perhaps in this tense atmosphere I developed an uncanny sixth sense, but I had a strange feeling this episode wasn't quite finished. I had no idea what was to come but I anticipated that more was to follow.

We were barely ten minutes into packing up when a messenger from Jayalalithaa walked in. I can't remember who it was. But I won't forget what he had to say.

'Amma wants to do the interview again.' She wasn't asking, she was merely informing us. It almost felt like an order.

Despite my apprehension and even nervousness, I felt I couldn't agree. I knew we had a good interview which would be riveting to watch. There was no need to do it again and, more importantly, any second attempt wouldn't be as gripping. And I certainly wasn't going to give up what felt like a winner for something that would be comparatively placid.

Amma, however, wasn't willing to take no for an answer. A series of messengers followed, not just to repeat and emphasize the request but also to point out that Jayalalithaa was unhappy and upset. The implied hint was that only if we did the interview again would she forgive and forget what had happened.

I was in my forties then and this felt like a challenge to my journalistic integrity. My thoughts were full of self-righteous defiance. Just because someone important is unhappy and wants to do another interview, should I agree? And if I did, wouldn't I be letting down the very principles I claim to stand up for?

Amma, I sensed, thought I might crumble under pressure and that made me yet more determined to stick to my refusal.

Was I right to take this rigid stand? After all, there had been earlier occasions when I had redone interviews. The one with Ram Jethmalani was redone at my own request. On other occasions, some had been repeated at the interviewee's request. At the time this had not perturbed me. So was I making a fuss for no good reason at all?

The truthful answer is probably yes. It's hard to say when you will dig in your toes and when you might choose to be more accommodating. On either occasion there's always an element of the unpredictable or, even, idiosyncratic. This time, as far as Amma was concerned, I was determined to be difficult.

To bolster my position, I decided to ring the BBC and ask the commissioning editor, Narendra Morar, for his advice. I felt confident he would agree that there were no grounds for redoing the interview.

However, once he heard the full story and the fact that we were still at Fort St George, Narendra feared we might not be able to get away if we kept saying no. They might just hold us back. Although he never used the word, perhaps he feared we could become hostages.

'I leave this one to you,' he said. 'You're the man on the spot. You must decide what's right. I'll stand by whatever you do. But for God's sake, stay safe. Let's not make a bad situation even worse.'

We must have been at Fort St George for at least an hour and a half after the interview ended. All that time we were in 'negotiation' with Amma's emissaries. But finally, our bags packed and our interlocutors exhausted, her officials accepted that no was no. We got up to leave and they let us.

As we drove out of Fort St George, Ashok turned to me, the tapes of the interview firmly in his hands, and said, 'We better make the most of this interview because Jayalalithaa will never give you another one again.'

Although at the time I was convinced he was right, Amma proved that Ashok was decidedly wrong. Either because she was a great politician or a generous and large-hearted woman, she took me completely by surprise when we next met.

It happened two years later at a National Integration Council meeting in Vigyan Bhawan, New Delhi. I was talking to Odisha Chief Minister Naveen Patnaik when she walked up and joined us. I assumed it was Naveen she wished to meet, not me, so I stepped aside.

'Where are you going, Karan?' she said in a voice that sounded genuinely cheerful. 'I came to talk to you. I meet Mr Patnaik all the time.'

I was stumped. I couldn't believe what I'd heard. Indeed, I stared back in silence, not knowing what to say. 'Well,' she said, smiling, her eyes twinkling with mirth, 'aren't you going to say something?'

'I wasn't sure you wanted to meet me,' I stammered. 'Have you forgotten our last meeting?'

'Of course,' she said and laughed. 'In fact, isn't it time for another?' But before I could answer she turned to Naveen and asked how he was. I took this as my cue to leave.

That second interview never happened. I'm not sure if I ever wrote and asked for it. Quite possibly I did not. But the warm-hearted and charming way she put the first behind us left as deep and lasting an impression as the abrasiveness of our original meeting.

It just proves how great politicians ensure they leave behind the impression they want to.

17

WHY MODI WALKED OUT AND
THE BJP SHUNS ME

It's no secret that the Narendra Modi government does not think very highly of me. No doubt there's the odd minister whom I am friendly with—Arun Jaitley being the principle example—but the vast majority, with whom I used to get on extremely well, found reasons or excuses to shun me within a year of Mr Modi becoming prime minister. Men like Ravi Shankar Prasad, Prakash Javadekar and M. Venkaiah Naidu, who readily gave interviews as opposition leaders and even during the first year or so after 2014, suddenly shut their doors. Some like Nirmala Sitharaman even went so far as to accept and set a date for the recording, only to back out at the last moment without explanation.

That I was persona non grata first became clear when BJP spokespersons started to refuse invitations to join discussions on my TV programmes. Initially, I assumed they were busy. However, when this kept repeating itself, I asked Sambit Patra if there was a problem. In a hushed voice and a manner that suggested he was embarrassed, he asked if I could keep a secret before he answered. When I gave him the necessary assurance, he said that all BJP spokespersons had been told not to appear on my shows.

Next were the ministers. From people who were always willing to be interviewed and who enjoyed a challenging exchange, they transformed into telephone numbers that refused to return calls. Their secretaries had only one answer: 'Sir says sorry. He's busy.'

The only person I could convince to appear on my show was Prakash Javadekar. He continued to do so well after his party spokespersons or his ministerial colleagues had made a habit of saying no or just not replying. Then one day, he too had second thoughts. I knew this was the case when he rang and asked, '*Meri party aapse kyun naraz hai*? What's happened, Karan? I've been told I mustn't give you an interview.'

This was the first time I was formally told that the BJP had a problem with me. Javadekar did not swear me to secrecy. Instead, he seemed surprised by the instruction that I was to be boycotted. He had rung to give me advice on how to handle the situation. '*Aap adyaksh-ji se milein aur isko sort out karen* (Meet the president and sort this out).'

Because I knew him, my first point of call was Arun Jaitley. I asked to meet him at the finance ministry where he assured me there wasn't a problem. He said I was imagining it. Everything, he said, would be okay.

I guess Arun was just being polite because the boycott continued. So I got in touch again. This time on the phone. Now he stopped denying there was a problem and, instead, told me that it would blow over. 'But Arun,' I responded, 'if it's going to blow over, that means there is something that has to blow away. So there is a problem.' Arun merely laughed.

I sensed that whatever the problem was, it was more than Arun could handle. I didn't and still do not doubt his offer or willingness to help but I did come to believe that he lacked the ability to do so.

If there was still room for any doubt, it was finally dispelled by BJP General Secretary Ram Madhav. I asked him for an interview in early January 2017 and, to my surprise and delight, he agreed. The recording was on 16 January. Afterwards, when I thanked him, his response left me – and my producer Arvind Kumar – stunned.

'You may say thank you,' he said, smiling but nonetheless serious, 'but my colleagues won't [thank me]. They don't think I should have agreed. They won't be happy that I've done this interview, but I don't believe we should boycott people.'

This was when I decided to meet Amit Shah. After I wrote a series of letters and phoned several times, he agreed to meet me the day after Holi in 2017. The meeting happened at his residence on Akbar Road. It wasn't a long one but sufficient for me to make my point and for him to respond.

I told him I had come to meet him because, over the last year, first BJP spokespersons and then BJP ministers had started refusing to appear on my programmes. I added that some spokespersons had actually told me in confidence that they had been forbidden from appearing and that, more recently, senior ministers had said the same thing. I also told him about Javadekar and my conversations with Arun Jaitley. Finally, I said I had come to find out what the problem was and, if I had unwittingly upset someone or said something, I would have no hesitation in apologizing. But what had I done?

Amit Shah listened to me in silence. I don't think I took more than a minute or two to explain.

We were sitting in the large drawing room of his house. He was in an armchair overlooking the garden; I on a sofa by his side. We were the only two people in the room.

'Karan-ji,' he said. He sounded friendly or, at least, there was no trace of the opposite either in his tone or manner. He claimed I had misunderstood the situation. He insisted that no instructions had been given to spokespersons or ministers to boycott my shows.

Finally, he promised to ring me in twenty-four hours after looking further into the matter.

I left feeling reassured and confident that whatever the problem, it had been resolved. I was terribly wrong.

Amit Shah never got back. Over the next six weeks I must have written a score of letters and telephoned and left messages perhaps fifty times. I got no response at all. But something did happen: the penny, at last, was beginning to drop.

Amit Shah's failure to respond made me think long and hard. I didn't think he was the sort of man who speaks casually and holds out false hope. Something or someone had stopped him. That's when I started to believe that the problem was probably Narendra Modi.

The more I thought about it, the more certain I felt of this. I had no proof—at least not at that point—but what else could explain BJP spokespersons suddenly refusing invitations, ministers agreeing and cancelling interviews, Javadekar's and Jaitley's comments and behaviour and, finally, Amit Shah's sudden silence after promising to get back in twenty-four hours?

Was the problem the interview I had done with Mr Modi in 2007, during the campaign for his second term as chief minister of Gujarat, when he had walked out after barely three minutes? Possibly, but I suspected that it went a little further back. And it didn't take long to realize that the roots must lie in a 'Sunday Sentiments' column I wrote in March 2002, days after the Godhra tragedy and the horrific killing of innocent Muslims that had followed.

I decided that perhaps it was time to speak to Mr Modi directly. Maybe an honest conversation would clear the air between us. Even if I half-felt this was unlikely, I thought it was worth the effort. So I rang his national security adviser, Ajit Doval, and also his principal secretary, Nripendra Misra.

I got to speak to Mr Misra before I met Mr Doval. Both conversations happened on the same day, 1 May 2017.

Nripendra Misra rang up in response to the message I had left in his office. I told him I wanted to meet Mr Modi to find out why I was being boycotted by his ministers and his party, and added that if I had unwittingly done something to upset the prime minister I was happy to apologize. But I first needed to know what that was. I also said I couldn't believe this was because of the interview I did in 2007 because that was now ten years ago.

Misra said he would have a word with Modi and get back to me. Later that evening, I called on Ajit Doval in South Block and repeated the same message. He said he would wait for Nripendra Misra to get back to me. He hoped that Misra would be able to sort out matters. But if he couldn't, Doval said he would have a word directly with Narendra Modi.

Three days later, Nripendra Misra rang. He said he had spoken to Modi and got the feeling there would be no point in my meeting the prime minister. He said the prime minister felt I was prejudiced against him and it was unlikely that my attitude would change. Misra also added that this was why Amit Shah had never got back. He too, presumably, had spoken to Modi and got a similar response.

I then rang Doval although I knew nothing further would be possible. I told him what Misra had said. He heard me out in silence. His only response was, 'Let's hope things clear up, but it will take time.'

So now I knew the cause of the problem. I had offended Narendra Modi and this was the result. The only thing I still wasn't sure of is when precisely that offence had happened. Was it the interview in 2007 or was it earlier with my 'Sunday Sentiments' column of March 2002? I suspect it had built up over the years but the start was probably with the column.

So, if I'm right in my hunch that this was when the problem began, then the fairest thing would be to repeat what I had written at the time. I called the article 'Go, Mr Modi, and go now'. This is what it said:

I thought I knew Narendra Modi. Not so long ago I respected him and was grateful for his advice. In 2000, when I was preparing for an interview with the RSS Sarsanghchalak, he helped me understand the organization and opened my eyes to its weaknesses. With perfect impartiality he made me aware of the damning mediocrity that has come to characterize its functioning.

'Question Sudarshan-ji about the RSS's loss of relevance. No longer does it stand for excellence. Today, it's mediocre in everything it does.' That's how he started the discussion.

'What do you mean?' I questioned. This was the last thing I expected to hear. After all, Modi is an RSS pracharak. I had sought him out as a defender of the Sangh, not as a critic.

'The RSS runs 20,000 schools and fifty papers. But none of these have achieved any measure of national distinction. The RSS is dedicated to social work but Sai Baba, the Radha Soami sect and Pandurang Athavale's Swadhyaya Group have bigger names in this field. The RSS doesn't count.'

I was stunned. Not simply because Mr Modi was being critical. More because he was offering a line of attack that came from within the RSS. This was not the traditional and hackneyed left [wing] critique. It was the searing disillusionment of the right. It was new. It was different.

'Ask him about the attendance at RSS shakhas,' Modi continued. I could sense his enthusiasm. He was behaving like a journalist. I liked that. More importantly, I admired his honesty and was grateful for his advice.

'Just look at Kerala. The biggest RSS unit is there but its impact is minimal. Instead, everything the RSS dislikes is thriving. The communists, the Church and an economy that is dependent on foreign not swadeshi funds. That's how irrelevant the RSS has become.

'Ask Sudarshan-ji about all of this and you will touch on issues that matter to people like me. It will be a fantastic interview.'

I had intended to follow this advice. But foolishly I started the interview on a more conventional tack. We spoke about the RSS's commitment to a Hindu Rashtra, the Constitution, the BJP's alliances and the Vajpayee government's performance. Then we ran out of time. Mr Modi's questions got squeezed out.

Even though many praised the interview and the press were kind to it, I knew it could have been better. It ought to have been different. It might even have been original. Had I found a way of incorporating Mr Modi's questions it would have been.

At the time I thought of Narendra Modi as a man who had the strength to question, the courage to challenge and the objectivity and generosity to share his sentiments across political divides. I can't pretend I knew much more about him. I certainly did not get to know him well. But I felt I did not need to. I liked—in fact, I admired—what I had seen. That was enough.

Sadly, it seems I was mistaken. No, that's not quite right. It's not being fully honest. The word 'seems' suggests a doubt or hesitation that is misplaced. The word 'mistaken' feels euphemistic. The truth is I was horribly wrong.

The image of Narendra Modi that emerges from his handling of the recent communal carnage in Gujarat is completely different. The 'other' Modi is narrow-minded, sectarian, mean-spirited and a prisoner of his limitations.

I can accept that his inexperience, maybe even his foolish personal pride, was the reason why the army was not called out earlier. Perhaps he thought he could handle the situation differently yet still effectively, show toughness but also a measure of understanding. After all, it's not easy to crack down on your own constituents, on those who share your beliefs. Even if tragic, such mistakes are human. They happen often enough.

But when he claims that for every action there will be a reaction, when he attempts to explain the murder of Ehsan Jafri by alluding to the fact that the mob was fired upon and when he finds grounds for paying the victims of Godhra double the amount paid to those who died in Ahmedabad, he reveals himself as a moral dwarf. To value a Hindu life more than a Muslim one or talk of mass murder as if it was somehow explicable is not just beyond comprehension—it's hateful.

The man I thought I knew was a leader. He had the spirit and the wisdom to rise above narrow confines, to turn opponents into friends, to win admiration from journalists, to guide and be followed. The man I discovered last week is a mere creature—of prejudice, of petty vengeance, of double standards and forked-tongued utterances.

The first Mr Modi deserved to be chief minister. The second deserves to be sacked.

Today, as I read what I had written seventeen years ago, in the light of all that has since happened, I can see how it would have caused offence. I was blunt and sharply critical. Clearly I had hit where it was likely to hurt most.

It was over five years later, in 2007, that my interview with Narendra Modi happened. If I recall correctly, I had asked Arun Jaitley for help and I'm sure it was his intervention that convinced the Gujarat chief minister to agree. The interview was arranged for an October afternoon in Ahmedabad and I arrived by the early morning flight. It was the morning after Benazir Bhutto's dramatic return to Karachi after years in exile and the terrible bomb blast that had shattered her procession, leaving hundreds dead. That, rather than the interview that was scheduled for later in the day, was at the top of my mind when the plane touched down in Ahmedabad.

I had just about got into the car and we were still within the airport's perimeter when my phone rang. '*Karan-ji, pahunch gaye?*' It was Narendra Modi ringing to welcome me. This was the first sign of how careful he is about handling the media.

'*Apna interview toh char baje hain lekin thoda pahle aana, gup-shup karenge* (Our interview is at 4 but come a little early, let's chat).'

Everything about his manner seemed to reassure me that Narendra Modi had either not read or forgotten about the column I wrote in 2002. He greeted me warmly and chatted as if I was an old friend. We didn't bring up any subject that the interview was likely to cover. Instead, we bantered, laughed and joked.

I wasn't sure if this was meant to disarm me. Canny politicians often resort to such guile. But certainly, any apprehensions I may have had quickly disappeared.

Half an hour later, we sat down in front of the cameras. Mr Modi was wearing a pale yellow kurta. His hair was freshly cut.

My first set of questions were about 2002. My intention was to get this tricky subject over with and then proceed to other matters. Not to have raised it at all would have looked like collusion or pusillanimity. Equally, however, I didn't want to make a meal of it. Hence, the decision to raise it and get it out of the way quickly.

'Mr Modi, let's start by talking about you,' is how I began. 'In the six years that you have been the chief minister of Gujarat, the Rajiv Gandhi Foundation has declared Gujarat to be the best administered state. *India Today*, on two separate occasions, has declared that you are the most efficient chief minister. And yet despite that, people still call you to your face a mass murderer and they accuse you of being prejudiced against Muslims. Do you have an image problem?'

He didn't seem at all flustered. I didn't notice any emotion on his face. Not even a change in his expression. It remained placid and unaffected. However, what did surprise me was that he chose to respond in English. Although today his command of the language is near-fluent, in 2007 it was not.

'I think it's not proper to say that "people". There are two or three persons, those who used to talk in this terminology and I always say God bless them.'

'You are saying this is a conspiracy of two-three people only?'

'I have not said so.'

'But you are saying it's only two-three people.'

'This is what I have information. It's not the people's voice.'

The truth is that the chief minister wasn't right in saying that only two or three people had spoken about him in this way. The judges of the Supreme Court of India, including the chief justice, had made observations in open court that amounted to precisely this. So I proceeded to question him on that.

'Can I point out to you that in September 2003, the Supreme Court said they had lost faith in the Gujarat government? In April 2004, the chief justice of the Supreme Court in open court said that you were like a modern-day Nero who looks the other side when helpless children and innocent women are burnt. The Supreme Court seems to have a problem with you.'

'Karan, I have a small request. Please go to the Supreme Court judgment. Is anything in writing? I'll be happy to know everything.'

'It wasn't in writing. You are absolutely right. It was an observation.'

'If it is in judgment, then I'll be happy to give you the answer.'

'But do you mean a criticism in court by the chief justice doesn't matter?'

'This is my simple request to you. Please go to the court judgment. Find out the sentence which you are quoting and I will be happy that if the people of India should know it.'

'It wasn't just an open comment made by the chief justice. In August 2004, the Supreme Court reopened over 2,100 cases out of a total of around 4,600—over 40 per cent—and they did so because they believed justice hadn't happened in Modi's Gujarat.'

'I'll be happy and I am happy because of this judgment because, ultimately, the court of law will take the decision.'

Mr Modi was making a legitimate distinction between what is formally written in a court's judgment and what is merely spoken obiter dicta in open court. However, for a politician seeking election, this was not a convincing defence. If the chief justice has criticized you, it hardly matters whether it was done in writing or verbally. More importantly, the criticism had been carried by all the papers on their front pages. This was, therefore, at the core of the image problem Modi faced as he campaigned for his second re-election. No amount of verbal jugglery could diminish that. And that was the point I was trying to put to him.

In fact, the truth is—sadly and foolishly, I did not know this at that time—the modern-day Nero comment I had quoted was not spoken verbally, as the newspapers of the time had suggested, but was part of a formal written judgment delivered by the Supreme Court. Teesta Setalvad gave me the details after watching the three-minute interview. In its judgment in the *Zahira Habibulla H. Sheikh v. State of Gujarat* case, delivered on 12 April 2004 by a bench comprising Justices Doraiswamy Raju and Arijit Pasayat and written by the latter, this is what the Supreme Court put in writing: 'The modern-day "Neros" were looking elsewhere when Best Bakery and innocent children and helpless women were burning, and were probably deliberating how the perpetrators of the crime can be saved or protected.' To be honest, this was even more damning than what I had claimed was only said orally. The written version also accused Mr Modi of 'probably deliberating how the perpetrators of the crime can be saved or protected'.

Alas, I was unaware of this when I was interviewing Mr Modi and so my question was weaker than it might have been. But even the diluted version was enough to rile him.

'I'll tell you what the problem is,' I continued in the interview. 'Even five years after the Gujarat killings of 2002, the ghost of Godhra still haunts you. Why have you not done more to allay that ghost?'

'This [task] I give it to media persons like Karan Thapar. Let them enjoy.'

'Can I suggest something to you?'

'I have no problem.'

'Why can't you say that you regret the killings that happened? Why can't you say maybe the government should have done more to protect Muslims?'

'What I have to say I have said at that time, and you can find out my statements.'

'Just say it again.'

'Not necessary I have to talk about in 2007 everything you want to talk about.'

'But by not saying it again, by not letting people hear the message repeatedly, you are allowing an image that is contrary to the interest of Gujarat to continue. It's in your hands to change it.'

Right through the two or three minutes this exchange lasted, Narendra Modi's face remained expressionless. But it was also clear he wasn't happy. His eyes were cold and hard. Perhaps he was making an effort to keep his face calm and steady. But now his patience or, perhaps, his resolve snapped. He had had enough and ended the interview. With the words 'I have to rest. I need some water' he started to take the microphone off.

At first I thought he was genuinely thirsty and pointed out that a glass of water was on a small table by his side. However, it didn't take long to realize that this was just an excuse. The interview was definitely over.

Yet even then Modi did not show any anger or even nastiness. The tape of these three minutes, which CNN-IBN repeatedly broadcast the next day, has Modi saying: '*Apni dosti bani rahe. Bas.* I'll be happy. You came here. I am happy and thankful to you. I can't do this interview ... *Aapke ideas hain, aap bolte rahiye, aap karte rahiye* ... *Dekho mein dostana sambhand banana chahta hoon* (They are your ideas, you keep speaking ... I want to maintain friendly relations with you).'

The odd part is that I must have spent at least an hour thereafter with him. He plied me with tea, mithai and Gujarati dhoklas. In these difficult circumstances, his hospitality was exceptional.

I spent that time trying hard to convince him to continue. I offered to redo the interview and put the questions about 2002 at the end. I assured him that I had many other matters to raise and only started with Godhra and the Muslim killings because, for both of us, it would have been wrong to avoid the subject. It was best to get it out of the way at the start.

None of this logic worked with Narendra Modi. I then said that if he left me with just three minutes the channel would show it repeatedly the next day. It would be treated like a news story. It would probably feature in every single bulletin. On the other hand, if he did the full interview, it would be broadcast once and repeated once and then forgotten, probably forever. But even this didn't work.

Modi kept saying that his mood had changed. He said he would do the interview some other time. But, simultaneously, he also repeated we must be friends. '*Dosti bani rahe,*' which he had said earlier, was repeated again and again.

When an hour was over, I said I had to leave otherwise I would miss the plane to Delhi. We shook hands and I departed.

The following Sunday the channel released the interview and it instantly became a headline story. As I had predicted, it featured in every bulletin. Modi's walking out was big news and because it happened in the middle of the Gujarat campaign, the Congress party made merry with it.

On Monday afternoon Modi called. '*Mere kandhe pe bandook rakh ke aap goli mar rahe ho.*' I said this was exactly what I had predicted. Indeed, this was why I'd felt he should have finished the interview rather than walk out.

Modi laughed. I will never forget what he then said.

'Karan brother, I love you. *Jab main Delhi aaonga bhojan karenge* (We'll have a meal together when I'm in Delhi).'

The truth is that these were just clever parting words. I've never met Mr Modi since. We've not even spoken. And there is no question of being invited to share a meal.

However—and this is important—for the next ten years after this interview it did not affect my relationship with the BJP in any way. To begin with, most of the party's senior leaders wanted to personally hear the story and I have to admit that I enjoyed telling them. More importantly, none were put off from giving interviews or, even, reluctant to agree.

This was the case from 2007 right up till 2015 or, possibly, early 2016. Even during the first year or eighteen months of Narendra Modi's government, the BJP's attitude towards me did not change. Its spokespersons and ministers always agreed to appear on my shows or grant interviews. It was as if the interview had never happened or was forgotten, as it deserved to be because by 2014 it was seven years old.

This is why when the period of 'untouchability' began I was initially unwilling to accept that it was because of the interview. Indeed, it took me a while to realize that that was in fact the case. Then, on 18 October 2017, Pavan Varma, the well-known diplomat, author and politician, gave me proof. What he said corroborated the impression Nripendra Misra had given me. The story Pavan told me was clinching.

Sitting in my office, his eyes happened to fall on a photograph of Narendra Modi. It was one of a group of former prime ministers whom I've interviewed. The Modi picture, however, was grabbed from the television screen and it's the precise moment that he starts to take off his mike and end the interview. A CNN-IBN caption, which was visible on screen, is part of the photograph. It says: 'Can't do this interview.'

'Do you know what Prashant Kishor told me about that interview?' Pavan suddenly asked. 'He said he had made Modi watch it thirty times as he prepared him for the 2014 elections. His team used your interview to teach Modi how to handle difficult questions or awkward uncomfortable moments.'

What followed was even more surprising as Pavan gave me further details of his conversation with Prashant Kishor. Modi told Prashant that he deliberately kept me for a whole hour after the interview so that I would leave his home convinced there were no ill feelings on his side. The cups of tea, mithai and dhokla were part of a strategy to disarm me. When I told Pavan that Modi had been extremely friendly and seemed by no means upset by the outcome of the interview, Pavan said this was deliberate. It was conscious strategy.

'But do you know something else?' Pavan added. 'Modi said to Prashant that he will never forgive you and when he gets an opportunity he will take his revenge. This is something Prashant repeated at least two or three times. It wasn't just an occasional comment made by Modi. Prashant was convinced that this was Modi's intent and he wouldn't rest till he had got even with you.'

I have no reason to disbelieve Pavan. He has nothing to gain by misleading me or even embellishing the truth. More importantly, what he said seemed to explain the way the BJP has treated me since around early 2016. This, no doubt, is why party spokespersons have been told not to appear on my programmes, why ministers started to decline interviews and, ultimately, why Amit Shah, after his initial reassurance, failed to get back or even take my calls. Perhaps this is also why, when Nripendra Misra spoke to him, Modi refused to meet me and resolve matters.

EPILOGUE

At the end there's only one question left to answer: why did I write this book?

It's not that I see myself at the end of my career and feel an urge to reflect in retirement. I still believe I have many active years ahead of me. Nor am I itching to tell my story. After all, I have shared aspects of my life with readers of the *Hindustan Times* for over two decades. A lot that I wanted to say has already been expressed in my weekly 'Sunday Sentiments' columns, albeit in fledgling form.

So why did I write this book? The truth is stark and simple. I had time on my hands and this felt like an easy, even an interesting, way of occupying myself.

Let me go one step further. A second truth is that this book was started on a whim. It wasn't planned and it certainly wasn't structured. Nor did I think carefully about how I would write about myself. It literally just happened once it began.

One afternoon in September 2017 I asked my long-suffering secretary, Santosh Kumar, to join me in my room and started dictating this book. This is why I say it began on a whim. I wasn't certain how far it would go or even where it would end. It just kept happening.

On some days I would dictate a few hundred words, on others several thousand. Santosh would type them up and I, in turn, would edit, correct and ensure the content had a sense of flow.

Readability was my key concern. Since I was relying on my memory, I was confident that only those moments that would be of wider interest would be covered. The pedestrian would not be recalled because they were forgotten.

Since I have a pretty good memory, I was also confident that my recollections were accurate. Occasionally, I would have to check facts and, sometimes, my earlier 'Sunday Sentiments' columns to ensure the lapse of time was not leading to unintended error.

Yet the funny thing is, when you begin to look back on your life, you start remembering things you had forgotten. The past comes tumbling back just because you're making an effort to recall it. One thing leads to another and a picture that has slipped out of memory suddenly forms itself all over again.

It's a bit like reliving your life a second time. Except this time, you do so with the benefit of hindsight, which means with the advantage of knowing how each episode will end. The danger, of course, is that you recapitulate what's happened in the light of your knowledge of how it will culminate. In other words, you write the finale into the telling.

I'm sure I've done that. Probably many times. But the truth is, it also makes it easier to understand events that otherwise, as they were happening, were neither logical nor explicable. They were just events. It's only when you look back that you can see the thread that connects them and, in the process, gives them meaning.

Now, as I said, most people write their books, type them or feed them into a computer. I chose the lazy option of dictation. But it had one unforeseen and even unintended advantage. I could hear myself speak as I dictated and discovered that this gave me the ability to assess how it would 'sound in the head' of any future reader. My voice provided me a second filter of judgement.

Finally, this book didn't take long to write. Most of it was over before Christmas 2017. The last few chapters were written the following January. This means that in the space of five months the book was done.

I hope all of the above explains the idiosyncratic and, often, self-focused character of the stories I have to tell. In fact, what I've done is relate different stories connected with my life. After the initial chapters, I've deliberately focused on events or episodes connected with the famous and I've had the good fortune of knowing several. Their roles in these stories make the latter more interesting. They also, I hope, reveal something about the people in them.

Of course, in the first instance, this book tells you about me, but I also hope it says something of people as different and varied as Lal Krishna Advani and Barack Obama, Sachin Tendulkar and General Pervez Musharraf, Sharmila Tagore and Jeremy Thorpe, Benazir Bhutto and Kapil Dev.

The chapter on my differences with Narendra Modi, his party and government is one that I wrote with particular care and attention to detail. Here I did not rely simply on memory. I made the additional effort of cross-checking my story as carefully as I could.

I know that at the end of that particular tale I have relied on what Pavan Varma told me. But I have no reason to disbelieve him. And what he said was spoken without any prompting on my part. I believe what he told me, which is why I have recounted it in the words that he used.

If this book has a beginning and a middle but just ends without seeming to there's a very simple and, indeed, truthful explanation I can offer. My life is not over! The end has not been reached. The book is done but life continues. I'm greatly looking forward to the years to come.

A FINAL WORD

I want to thank Santosh Kumar sincerely for all his diligence and forbearance. I am not an easy person to have dictating copy. I am also grateful to Krishan Chopra for so readily accepting this book when I offered it to him, and to Amrita Mukerji, Bonita Vaz-Shimray, Rohit Chawla and Aman Arora for putting up with my crotchety behaviour. Even though I won't accept it, I have all the bad habits of a curmudgeonly old man!

To all of them, my thanks and apologies.

INDEX

Index

ABOUT THE AUTHOR

Karan Thapar worked for ten years in television in the UK, where he trained as a correspondent, producer, editor and presenter with London Weekend Television and worked on programmes as varied as *Weekend World, The World This Week, The Business Programme, The Walden Interview* and *Eastern Eye*. Prior to that, he worked as a foreign correspondent with *The Times*, London. After his return to India in 1991, he presented well-known programmes such as *Eyewitness* (Doordarshan), *HARDtalk India* (BBC), *Devil's Advocate* (CNN-IBN) and *To The Point* (India Today). He helped establish and headed HT Vision Ltd as executive producer, was director of programmes at Home TV and president, news and current affairs, at UTV. Presently, he is the President of Infotainment Television (ITV) and writes a weekly column, 'Sunday Sentiments', for the *Hindustan Times* and a fortnightly column, 'As I See It', for *Business Standard*.

In 2006 a collection of his columns in the *Hindustan Times* was published in a book called *Sunday Sentiments* (Wisdom Tree) and a compilation of his interviews for the BBC was published by Penguin Books India as a book called *Face to Face India*. In 2009 a second collection of his columns, *More Salt than Pepper*, was published by HarperCollins India. A third, called *As I Like It*, was published in 2018 (Wisdom Tree).

Karan Thapar has won several awards such as the Asian Television Award for Best Current Affairs Presenter (five-time winner), the Ramnath Goenka Broadcast Journalist of the Year Award (2009), the Indian News Broadcasting Award for the Best Current Affairs Presenter (2009 and 2010), the International Press Institute – India Award for Excellence in Journalism (2013) and the G. K. Reddy Award (2018).